G.W. Leibniz

Discourse on Metaphysics
and Other Essays

Discourse on Metaphysics
On the Ultimate Origination of Things
Preface to the *New Essays*
The Monadology

Edited and Translated by
Daniel Garber
and
Roger Ariew

Hackett Publishing Company
Indianapolis & Cambridge

For the next generation,
David, Elisabeth, Hannah, and Daniel

G. W. Leibniz, 1646–1716

19 18 17 16 15 14   5 6 7 8 9

Cover design by Listenberger Design & Associates
Interior design by Dan Kirklin

For further information, please address
   Hackett Publishing Company, Inc.
   P.O. Box 44937
   Indianapolis, Indiana 46244-0937

   www.hackettpublishing.com

Library of Congress Cataloging-in-Publication Data

Leibniz, Gottfried Wilhelm, Freiherr von, 1646–1716.
   [Selections. English. 1991]
   Discourse on metaphysics & other essays/G.W. Leibniz.
      p.   cm.
   Translated by Daniel Garber and Roger Ariew.
   Includes bibliographical references.
   Contents: Discourse on metaphysics—On the ultimate origination
of things—Preface to the New essays—Monadology.
   ISBN 0-87220-133-3 — ISBN 0-87220-132-5 (pbk.)
   1. Philosophy—Early works to 1800. I. Title. II. Title:
Discourse on metaphysics and other essays.
   [B2558.A74213   1991]
   110—dc20   91-24570
                                                    CIP

ISBN-13: 978-0-87220-133-0 (cloth)
ISBN-13: 978-0-87220-132-3 (pbk.)

Contents

Introduction

Leibniz: Life and Works

GOTTFRIED WILHELM LEIBNIZ was born on July 1, 1646, in Leipzig. His father, Friedrich, a scholar and a Professor of Moral Philosophy at the University of Leipzig, died in September 1652, when Leibniz was only six years old. But despite his father's early death, the younger Leibniz was later to recall how his father had instilled in him a love of learning. Learning was, indeed, to become an important part of his life. Leibniz began school when he was seven years old. Even so, he later describes himself as self-taught.[1] Leibniz seems to have taught himself Latin at age seven or eight, in order to read editions of Livy and Calvisius that fell into his hands; as a result, he was allowed admission into his late father's extensive library. There he read widely, but concentrated especially in the Church Fathers and in the Latin classics. Leibniz attended university from age fourteen to age twenty-one, first at the University of Leipzig (1661–1666) and then at the University of Altdorf (1666–1667), graduating with degrees in law and in philosophy. He was quickly recognized as a young man of great promise and talent and was invited to join the faculty at the University of Altdorf. He chose instead to go into public service. Under the patronage of Baron Johann Christian von Boineburg, Leibniz entered the service of the Elector of Mainz and occupied a number of positions in Mainz and nearby Nuremburg. There he stayed until he was sent to Paris in spring 1672 on diplomatic business, a trip that deeply affected his intellectual development.

The intellectual world of the late seventeenth century was very exciting indeed. The century began still very much under the influence of the Aristotelian philosophy that had dominated European thought since the 13th century, when the bulk of the Aristotelian corpus was rediscovered and translated from Greek and Arabic into Latin. But much had happened by the time Leibniz went to school. A new philosophy had emerged from figures like Galileo and his students, Torricelli and Cavalieri, from Descartes and his numerous camp, from Gassendi, Pascal, Hobbes, and from countless others.

1. See AG 6.

Not without a fight and not without hesitations, the substantial forms and primary matter of the schoolmen had given away to a new world, the mechanist world of geometrical bodies or atoms in motion. Together with this new world had come new mathematical tools for dealing with the new geometrical bodies. But this new world view raised new problems as well, including, among others, problems of necessity, contingency, and freedom in a world governed by laws of motion, problems connected with the place of the soul and its immortality, and problems concerning God and his creation, sustenance, and ends.

Leibniz knew little of the new philosophy before 1672. He was originally brought up in an older tradition of Aristotelian Scholasticism, supplemented with liberal doses of Renaissance humanism. He reports much later in life that he was converted to the new mechanism at age fifteen, in 1661 or 1662, presumably, and reports having given up Aristotle for the new philosophy.[2] But even so, he later confesses that the knowledge he had of the moderns was quite slim at that time, and despite his enthusiasm, the considerable amount of work he did in what he took to be the new philosophy was the work of an amateur.[3]

When in Paris from 1672 to 1676, Leibniz made his entrance into the learned world and did his best to seek out the intellectual luminaries that made Paris an important center of learning. Most important, he came to know Christiaan Huygens, under whose tutelage Leibniz was introduced to the moderns. Leibniz quickly progressed, and in those years he laid the foundations for his calculus, his physics, and the central core of what was to become his philosophy.

Before Leibniz returned to Germany in December 1676, he stopped in England and in Holland, where he met Spinoza. Both Boineburg and the Elector of Mainz had died while he was in Paris. Leibniz returned to the court of Hanover as a counselor. Though he often traveled and took on responsibilities elsewhere, Hanover was to be his main home for the rest of his life. Leibniz took on a wide variety of tasks, both for the court at Hanover and for his numerous other employers. He served as a mining engineer, unsuccessfully supervising the draining of the silver mines in the Harz mountains, as the head librarian over a vast collection of books and manuscripts, as an advisor and diplomat, and as a court historian. In this later capacity, Leibniz wrote a geological history of the region of Lower Saxony, the *Protogaea*, that proved to be an important work in the

2. See Leibniz to Nicolas Remond, 10 January 1714, G III 606, translated in L 655.
3. See the letter to Foucher, AG 1–5. Some of his early physics is discussed in the "Specimen of Dynamics"; see AG 117–38.

history of geology when it was finally published in 1749, many years after his death. In this connection he also published a number of volumes of the historical documents he found in the archives he combed, looking for material for his history, and he undertook some of the earliest research into European languages, their origins, and their evolution.

But all the while, through a succession of employers at Hanover and elsewhere, Leibniz continued to develop the philosophical system he had started in Paris and before, in a series of essays, letters, and two books. In metaphysics, the unpublished "Discourse on Metaphysics," composed in 1686 but anticipated in earlier writings, developed themes discussed in the letters to Arnauld written in that and the following years. Themes from the "Discourse" also appear, somewhat transformed, in the "New System of Nature," which Leibniz published in 1695—the first public exposition of his metaphysical system—and again in the unpublished essay "On the Ultimate Origination of Things" of 1697 and again in the important essay "On Nature Itself," published in 1698. These themes appear further transformed in the late summaries of his doctrines, the unpublished "Principles of Nature and Grace" and "Monadology." Behind the metaphysics of these essays is Leibniz's program for logic and a universal language, developed most conspicuously in a remarkable series of papers from the late 1670s and 1680s, in which he explicates the concept of truth which he draws upon in the celebrated characterization of the individual he gives in section 8 of the "Discourse." Leibniz was also deeply involved with the study of physics. The most extensive account of his physics is found in his *Dynamics* (1689–91), in which he sets out the basic laws of motion and force. This work was never published, but Leibniz was persuaded to publish an essay based on it. The essay "A Specimen of Dynamics" appeared in 1695; it contained a discussion of the metaphysical foundations of his physics. In the course of articulating and defending his own view, Leibniz differentiated his conception of physics from that of the Cartesians and the Newtonians and related his view to that of the schoolmen; to those ends he maintained an extensive circle of correspondents, including Huygens, De Volder, Des Bosses, and Clarke. Theology was a constant theme; it became central in the *Theodicy* of 1710, one of two philosophical books Leibniz wrote. His other philosophical book was the *New Essays on Human Understanding*, finished in 1704 but never published. The *New Essays* were meant as a response to Locke's *Essay Concerning Human Understanding*, but Locke's death in 1704 caused Leibniz to withhold publication. In general, Leibniz was an avid reader, reading and reacting to the thought of his contemporaries. In addition to the *New Essays* and other writings on Locke, Leibniz left detailed essays and notes on Hobbes and Spinoza, Descartes and Malebranche, Newton and even the very young George Berkeley, to name but a select few of those who caught Leibniz's attention.

It is natural enough to try to find order in this apparent chaos, to try to identify *the* Leibnizian doctrine of one thing or another, or to try to find the single key to Leibniz's thought, the premise from which everything follows neatly. No doubt this can be done, to some extent, and an orderly Leibnizian philosophy can be reconstructed from the somewhat disorderly notes Leibniz left. But it is also important to be sensitive to the sometimes subtle, sometimes not so subtle changes as Leibniz develops a doctrine, first trying one thing, then another, looking at the world of his philosophy from different points of view.[4] It is also important to appreciate not only the philosophical premises Leibniz uses, but also the different historical strands he attempts to weave together. Late in life Leibniz told one correspondent, Nicolas Remond, that he had always tried "to uncover and reunite the truth buried and scattered through the opinions of the different sects of philosophers." Leibniz continued: "I have found that most sects are correct in the better part of what they put forward, though not so much in what they deny. . . ."[5] In this way Leibniz hoped to unite Catholicism and Protestantism, Hobbesian materialism with Cartesian dualism, and the mechanism of the moderns with the substantial forms of the schoolmen.

Leibniz died in his bed in Hanover on November 14, 1716. The last of his many employers, Georg Ludwig, had been in London since succeeding to the throne of England as George I some two years earlier. But Leibniz was not welcome there. The official reason was that Leibniz was to stay in Hanover until the history of the House of Hanover was close to complete. But there was also great hostility at court to the then elderly counselor. Important too must have been the protracted debate between Leibniz and Newton over the priority of the discovery of the calculus, which had been going on for some years and had taken on decidedly nationalistic overtones. When Leibniz died in Hanover, what was left of the court failed to attend his otherwise proper funeral. But though his immediate fellows may not have appreciated him, he had already become extremely well known

---

4. For an elegant example of a study of Leibniz from this point of view, see Robert M. Adams, "Leibniz's Theories of Contingency," in Hooker, ed., *Leibniz*.
5. Leibniz to Remond, 10 January 1714, G III 607, translated in L 655.

and respected by the time of his death. He never founded a school
of thought, as Descartes before him had, but even after his death,
his works continued to be published and his views discussed.[6]

Selected Bibliography of the Works of Leibniz[7]

[G]:   Gerhardt, C.I. *G.W. Leibniz: Die philosophischen
          Schriften*, 7 vols. (Berlin, 1875–90).
[A]:   *G.W. Leibniz: Sämtliche Schriften und Briefe* (Darmstadt
          and Leipzig, 1923–).
[Gr]:   Grua, G. *G.W. Leibniz: Textes inédits d'après les manuscrits
          de la Bibliothèque provinciale de Hanovre* (Paris, 1948).
[RPM]:   Leibniz, G.W. (ed. A. Robinet). *Principes de la nature et
          de la grace fondés en raison, et, Principes de la philosophie
          ou monadologie* (Paris, 1954).
[LD]:   Leibniz, G.W. (ed. H. Lestienne). *Discours de Métaphy-
          sique* (Paris, 1975).
[VE]:   *Vorausedition zur Reihe VI—Philosophische Schriften—in
          der Ausgabe der Akademie der DDR* (Münster, 1982–).

For more detailed bibliographical information concerning Leibniz's
works, please consult E. Ravier, *Bibliographie des Oeuvres de Leibniz*
(reprinted Hildesheim: Olms, 1966), along with Paul Schrecker's
corrections and additions in his review, "Une bibliographie de Leibniz," *Revue philosophique de la France et de l'étranger* 63 (1938): 324–
46.

Selected Bibliography of Secondary Works

Belaval, Yvon. *Leibniz critique de Descartes* (Paris, 1960).
———. *Leibniz: Initiation à sa philosophie* (Paris, 1962).
Broad, C.D. *Leibniz: an Introduction* (Cambridge, 1975).
Brown, Stuart. *Leibniz* (Minneapolis, 1984).

6. For a fuller account of Leibniz's life and works, see E.J. Aiton, *Leibniz, A Biography*
(Bristol, 1985), and Kurt Müller and Gisela Krönert, *Leben und Werk von Gottfried
Wilhelm Leibniz: eine Chronik* (Frankfurt, 1969).
7. Original language texts consulted in the preparation of this translation.

Cassirer, Ernst. *Leibniz' System in seinen wissenschaftlichen Grundlagen* (Marburg, 1902).

Costabel, Pierre. *Leibniz and Dynamics* (Ithaca, N.Y., 1973).

Couturat, Louis. *La logique de Leibniz* (Paris, 1901).

Frankfurt, Harry (ed.). *Leibniz* (Garden City, N.Y., 1972).

Gueroult, Martial. *Leibniz: Dynamique et métaphysique* (Paris, 1967).

Hooker, Michael (ed.). *Leibniz: Critical and Interpretative Essays* (Minneapolis, 1982).

Ishiguro, Hidé. *Leibniz's Philosophy of Logic and Language* (Ithaca, N.Y., 1972).

Jalabert, Jacques. *Le dieu de Leibniz* (Paris, 1960).

———. *La théorie leibnizienne de la substance* (Paris, 1947).

Jolley, Nicholas. *Leibniz and Locke* (Oxford, 1984).

Loemker, Leroy. *Struggle for Synthesis: the Seventeenth Century Background of Leibniz's Synthesis of Order and Freedom* (Cambridge, Mass., 1972).

MacDonald Ross, George. *Leibniz* (Oxford, 1984).

McRae, Robert. *Leibniz: Perception, Apperception, and Thought* (Toronto, 1976).

Mates, Benson. *The Philosophy of Leibniz: Metaphysics and Language* (Oxford, 1986).

Okruhlik, K., and J.R. Brown (eds.). *The Natural Philosophy of Leibniz* (Dordrecht, 1985).

Parkinson, G.H.R. *Logic and Reality in Leibniz's Metaphysics* (Oxford, 1965).

Rescher, Nicholas. *Leibniz's Metaphysics of Nature* (Dordrecht, 1981).

———. *The Philosophy of Leibniz* (Englewood Cliffs, N.J., 1967).

Robinet, André. *Architectonique disjonctive automates systématiques et idealité transcendentale dans l'oeuvre de G.W. Leibniz* (Paris, 1986).

Russell, Bertrand. *A Critical Exposition of the Philosophy of Leibniz* (London, 1900).

Sleigh, Robert. *Leibniz and Arnauld* (New Haven, 1990).

Wilson, Catherine, *Leibniz's Metaphysics: A Historical and Comparative Study* (Princeton, 1989).

Woolhouse, R.S. (ed.). *Leibniz: Metaphysics and Philosophy of Science* (Oxford, 1981).

Translations and Other Texts
Referred to in the Notes

[AT]: Adam, C., and P. Tannery (eds.). *Oeuvres de Descartes* (Paris, 1897–1909; new ed., Paris, 1964–1974), 11 vols.

Bayle, Pierre (ed. and trans. R.H. Popkin). *Historical and Critical Dictionary: Selections* (Indianapolis, 1965).

[Ols]: Descartes, René (trans. Paul J. Olscamp). *Discourse on Method, Optics, Geometry, and Meteorology* (Indianapolis, 1965).

[AG]: Leibniz, G.W. (trans. R. Ariew and D. Garber). *Philosophical Essays* (Indianapolis, 1989).

[L]: ———. (trans. L. Loemker). *Philosophical Papers and Letters* (Dordrecht, 1969).

———. (trans. E.M. Huggard). *Theodicy* (La Salle, Ill., 1985).

———. (trans. P. Remnant and J. Bennett). *New Essays on Human Understanding* (Cambridge, 1981).

Locke, John. *Works* (London, 1824).

———. (ed. Nidditch). *An Essay Concerning Human Understanding* (Oxford, 1975).

Malebranche, Nicholas. *The Search after Truth* (trans. T.M. Lennon and P.J. Olscamp) and *Elucidations of the Search after Truth* (trans. T.M. Lennon) (Columbus, Ohio, 1980).

———. *Traité de la nature et de la grâce*, vol. IV of André Robinet, ed., *Oeuvres Complètes de Malebranche* (Paris, 1958–70).

Spinoza, Baruch (trans. Samuel Shirley). *The Ethics and Selected Letters* (Indianapolis, 1982).

Discourse on Metaphysics (1686)[8]

In February 1686, Leibniz wrote a letter to the Landgrave Ernst von Hessen-Reinfels, saying: "being somewhere having nothing to do for a few days, I have lately composed a short discourse on metaphysics. . . ." (G II, 11). The "short discourse" was not published or even circulated in Leibniz's lifetime, to the best of our knowledge; at best Leibniz seems to have circulated summaries of its sections to the great theologian and philosopher Antoine Arnauld, sparking a celebrated exchange of views. (See the Letters to Arnauld, AG 69–90.) But the work that resulted from these few days of leisure is generally regarded as one of the most important statements of Leibniz's mature thought, a summary of his metaphysical system as it appeared to him in that very productive decade.

1. On Divine Perfection, and That God Does Everything in the Most Desirable Way.

THE MOST widely accepted and meaningful notion we have of God is expressed well enough in these words, that God is an absolutely perfect being; yet the consequences of these words are not sufficiently considered. And, to penetrate more deeply into this matter, it is appropriate to remark that there are several entirely different perfections in nature, that God possesses all of them together, and that each of them belongs to him in the highest degree.

We must also know what a perfection is. A fairly sure test for being a perfection is that forms or natures that are not capable of a highest degree are not perfections, as for example, the nature of number or figure. For the greatest of all numbers (or even the number of all numbers), as well as the greatest of all figures, imply a contradiction, but the greatest knowledge and omnipotence do not involve any impossibility. Consequently, power and knowledge are perfections, and, insofar as they belong to God, they do not have limits.

Whence it follows that God, possessing supreme and infinite wisdom, acts in the most perfect manner, not only metaphysically, but also morally speaking, and that, with respect to ourselves, we can say that the more enlightened and informed we are about God's works, the more we will be disposed to find them excellent and in complete conformity with what we might have desired.

---

8. G IV 427–63 and LD. French.

1

2. Against Those Who Claim That There Is No Goodness in God's Works, or That the Rules of Goodness and Beauty Are Arbitrary.

THUS I AM far removed from the opinion of those who maintain that there are no rules of goodness and perfection in the nature of things or in the ideas God has of them and who say that the works of God are good solely for the formal reason that God has made them.[9] For, if this were so, God, knowing that he is their author, would not have had to consider them afterwards and find them good, as is testified by the Sacred Scriptures—which seem to have used such anthropomorphic expressions only to make us understand that the excellence of God's works can be recognized by considering them in themselves, even when we do not reflect on this empty external denomination which relates them to their cause. This is all the more true, since it is by considering his works that we can discover the creator. His works must therefore carry his mark in themselves. I confess that the contrary opinion seems to me extremely dangerous and very near to the opinion of the recent innovators[10] who hold that the beauty of the universe and the goodness we attribute to the works of God are but the chimeras of those who conceive of God in terms of themselves. Thus, in saying that things are not good by virtue of any rule of goodness but solely by virtue of the will of God, it seems to me that we unknowingly destroy all of God's love and all his glory. For why praise him for what he has done if he would be equally praiseworthy in doing the exact contrary? Where will his justice and wisdom reside if there remains only a certain despotic power, if will holds the place of reason, and if, according to the definition of tyrants, justice consists in whatever pleases the most powerful? Besides, it seems that all acts of will presuppose a reason for willing and that this reason is naturally prior to the act of will. That is why I also find completely strange the expression of some other philosophers[11] who say that the eternal truths of metaphysics and geometry and consequently also the rules of goodness, justice, and perfection are merely the effects of the will of God; instead, it seems to me, they are only the consequences of his understanding, which, assuredly, does not depend on his will, any more than does his essence.

---

9. This is Descartes's view. See, e.g., the *Sixth Replies*, AT VII 432, 435–36.

10. Spinoza, and by extension, Descartes. The earlier draft, as reported by Lestienne, explicitly mentions the Spinozists alone in this regard. See Spinoza, appendix to *Ethics*, part 1.

11. Descartes is mentioned in an earlier draft, but deleted.

3. Against Those Who Believe That God Might Have Made Things Better.

NOR CAN I approve of the opinion of some moderns who maintain boldly that what God has made is not of the highest perfection and that he could have done much better.[12] For it seems to me that the consequences of this opinion are wholly contrary to the glory of God: as a lesser evil is relatively good, so a lesser good is relatively evil. And to act with less perfection than one could have is to act imperfectly. To show that an architect could have done better is to find fault with his work. This opinion is also contrary to the Sacred Scripture, which assure us of the goodness of God's works. For, if their view were sufficient, then since the series of imperfections descends to infinity, God's works would always have been good in comparison with those less perfect, no matter how he created them but something is hardly praiseworthy if it can be praised only in this way. I also believe that a great many passages from Sacred Scripture and the holy fathers will be found favoring my opinion, but scarcely any will be found favoring the opinion of these moderns, an opinion which is, in my judgment, unknown to all antiquity and which is based only on the inadequate knowledge we have of the general harmony of the universe and of the hidden reasons for God's conduct. This enables us to judge audaciously that many things could have been rendered better. Besides, these moderns insist on certain dubious subtleties, for they imagine that nothing is so perfect that there is not something more perfect—this is an error.

They also believe that in this way they are able to safeguard God's freedom, as though it were not freedom of the highest sort to act in perfection following sovereign reason. For to believe that God does something without having any reason for his will—overlooking the fact that this seems impossible—is an opinion that conforms little to his glory. Let us assume, for example, that God chooses between A and B and that he takes A without having any reason to prefer it to B. I say that this action of God is at the very least not praiseworthy; for all praise must be based on some reason, and by hypothesis there is none here. Instead I hold that God does nothing for which he does not deserve to be glorified.

---

12. See, e.g., Malebranche, *Traité de la nature et de la grâce*, Pr. disc., sec. xiv. Malebranche's *Traité* seems to be one of the main targets of this essay.

4. That the Love of God Requires Our Complete Satisfaction and Acquiescence with Respect to What He Has Done without Our Being Quietists as a Result.

THE GENERAL KNOWLEDGE of this great truth, that God acts always in the most perfect and desirable way possible, is, in my judgment, the foundation of the love that we owe God in all things, since he who loves seeks his satisfaction in the happiness or perfection of the object loved and in his actions. To will the same and dislike the same is true friendship. And I believe that it is difficult to love God well when we are not disposed to will what God wills, when we might have the power to change it. In fact, those who are not satisfied with what God does seem to me like dissatisfied subjects whose attitudes are not much different from those of rebels.

I hold, therefore, that, according to these principles, in order to act in accordance with the love of God, it is not sufficient to force ourselves to be patient; rather, we must truly be satisfied with everything that has come to us according to his will. I mean this acquiescence with respect to the past. As for the future, we must not be quietists[13] and stand ridiculously with arms folded, awaiting that which God will do, according to the sophism that the ancients called *logon aergon*, the lazy reason. But we must act in accordance with what we presume to be the *will of God*, insofar as we can judge it, trying with all our might to contribute to the general good and especially to the embellishment and perfection of that which affects us or that which is near us, that which is, so to speak, in our grasp. For, although the outcome might perhaps demonstrate that God did not wish our good will to have effect at present, it does not follow that he did not wish us to act as we have. On the contrary, since he is the best of all masters, he never demands more than the right intention, and it is for him to know the proper hour and place for letting the good designs succeed.

5. What the Rules of the Perfection of Divine Conduct Consist in, and That the Simplicity of the Ways Is in Balance with the Richness of the Effects.

THEREFORE IT IS sufficient to have the confidence that God does everything for the best and that nothing can harm those who

---

13. The quietists were followers of Miguel de Molinos (ca. 1640–97), author of the *Guida spirituale* (1675), and others, who stressed passive contemplation and complete resignation to the will of God.

love him. But to know in detail the reasons that could have moved him to choose this order of the universe—to allow sins, to dispense his saving grace in a certain way—surpasses the power of a finite mind, especially when it has not yet attained the enjoyment of the vision of God.

However, we can make some general remarks concerning the course of providence in the governance of things. We can therefore say that one who acts perfectly is similar to an excellent geometer who can find the best constructions for a problem; or to a good architect who makes use of his location and the funds set aside for a building in the most advantageous manner, allowing nothing improper or lacking in the beauty of which it is capable; or to a good householder, who makes use of his holdings in such a way that there remains nothing uncultivated and sterile; or to a skilled machinist who produces his work in the least difficult way possible; or to a learned author who includes the greatest number of truths [realités] in the smallest possible volume. Now, the most perfect of all beings, those that occupy the least volume, that is, those that least interfere with one another, are minds, whose perfections consist in their virtues. That is why we mustn't doubt that the happiness of minds is the principal aim of God and that he puts this into practice to the extent that general harmony permits it. We shall say more about this below.

As for the simplicity of the ways of God, this holds properly with respect to his means, as opposed to the variety, richness, and abundance, which holds with respect to his ends or effects. And the one must be in balance with the other, as are the costs of a building and the size and beauty one demands of it. It is true that nothing costs God anything—even less than it costs a philosopher to build the fabric of his imaginary world out of hypotheses—since God has only to make decrees in order that a real world come into being. But in matters of wisdom, decrees or hypotheses take the place of expenditures to the extent that they are more independent of one another, because reason requires that we avoid multiplying hypotheses or principles, in somewhat the same way that the simplest system is always preferred in astronomy.

6. God Does Nothing Which Is Not Orderly and It Is Not Even Possible to Imagine Events That Are Not Regular.

THE VOLITIONS or acts of God are commonly divided into ordinary or extraordinary. But it is good to consider that God does nothing which is not orderly. Thus, what passes for extraordinary is extraordinary only with respect to some particular order established among creatures; for everything is in conformity with the universal order. This is true to such an extent that not only does nothing completely irregular occur in the world, but we would not even be able to imagine such a thing. Thus, let us assume, for example, that someone jots down a number of points at random on a piece of paper, as do those who practice the ridiculous art of geomancy.[14] I maintain that it is possible to find a geometric line whose notion is constant and uniform, following a certain rule, such that this line passes through all the points in the same order in which the hand jotted them down.

And if someone traced a continuous line which is sometimes straight, sometimes circular, and sometimes of another nature, it is possible to find a notion, or rule, or equation common to all the points of this line, in virtue of which these very changes must occur. For example, there is no face whose contours are not part of a geometric line and cannot be traced in one stroke by a certain regular movement. But, when a rule is extremely complex, what is in conformity with it passes for irregular.

Thus, one can say, in whatever manner God might have created the world, it would always have been regular and in accordance with a certain general order. But God has chosen the most perfect world, that is, the one which is at the same time the simplest in hypotheses and the richest in phenomena, as might be a line in geometry whose construction is easy and whose properties and effects are extremely remarkable and widespread. I use these comparisons to sketch an imperfect likeness of divine wisdom and to point out something that can at least elevate our minds to conceive in some way what cannot be sufficiently expressed. But I do not claim to explain in this way the great mystery upon which the entire universe depends.

7. That Miracles Conform to the General Order, Even Though They May Be Contrary to the Subordinate Maxims; and about What God Wills or Permits by a General or Particular Volition.

NOW, since nothing can happen which is not in the order, one can say that miracles are as much within the order as are natural

---

14. Geomancy is the art of divination by means of lines or figures.

operations, operations which are called natural because they are in conformity with certain subordinate maxims that we call the nature of things. For one can say that this nature is only God's custom, with which he can dispense for any stronger reason than the one which moved him to make use of these maxims.

As for the general or particular volitions, depending upon how the matter is understood, we can say that God does everything following his most general will, which is in conformity with the most perfect order he has chosen, but we can also say that he has particular volitions which are exceptions to these aforementioned subordinate maxims. For the most general of God's laws, the one that rules the whole course of the universe, is without exception.

We can say also that God wills everything that is an object of his particular volition. But we must make a distinction with respect to the objects of his general volition, such as the actions of other creatures, particularly the actions of those that are reasonable, actions with which God wishes to concur. For, if the action is good in itself, we can say that God wills it and sometimes commands it, even when it does not take place. But if the action is evil in itself and becomes good only by accident, because the course of things (particularly punishment and atonement) corrects its evilness and repays the evil with interest in such a way that in the end there is more perfection in the whole sequence than if the evil had not occurred, then we must say that God permits this but does not will it, even though he concurs with it because of the laws of nature he has established and because he knows how to draw a greater good from it.

8. To Distinguish the Actions of God from Those of Creatures We Explain the Notion of an Individual Substance.

IT IS RATHER DIFFICULT to distinguish the actions of God from those of creatures; for some believe that God does everything, while others imagine that he merely conserves the force he has given to creatures. What follows will let us see the extent to which we can say the one or the other. And since actions and passions properly belong to individual substances [*actiones sunt suppositorum*],[15] it will be necessary to explain what such an individual substance is.

It is indeed true that when several predicates are attributed to a

---

15. Leibniz is making use of Scholastic logical terminology: a *suppositum* is an individual subsistent substance; *actiones sunt suppositorum* therefore means that actions are of individual subsistent substances.

single subject and this subject is attributed to no other, it is called an individual substance; but this is not sufficient, and such an explanation is merely nominal. We must therefore consider what it is to be attributed truly to a certain subject.

Now it is evident that all true predication has some basis in the nature of things and that, when a proposition is not an identity, that is, when the predicate is not explicitly contained in the subject, it must be contained in it virtually. That is what the philosophers call *in-esse*, when they say that the predicate is in the subject. Thus the subject term must always contain the predicate term, so that one who understands perfectly the notion of the subject would also know that the predicate belongs to it.

Since this is so, we can say that the nature of an individual substance or of a complete being is to have a notion so complete that it is sufficient to contain and to allow us to deduce from it all the predicates of the subject to which this notion is attributed. An accident, on the other hand, is a being whose notion does not include everything that can be attributed to the subject to which the notion is attributed.[16] Thus, taken in abstraction from the subject, the quality of being a king which belongs to Alexander the Great is not determinate enough to constitute an individual and does not include the other qualities of the same subject, nor does it include everything that the notion of this prince includes. On the other hand, God, seeing Alexander's individual notion or haecceity,[17] sees in it at the same time the basis and reason for all the predicates which can be said truly of him, for example, that he vanquished Darius and Porus; he even knows *a priori* (and not by experience) whether he died a natural death or whether he was poisoned, something we can know only through history. Thus when we consider carefully the connection of things, we can say that from all time in Alexander's soul there are vestiges of everything that has happened to him and marks of everything that will happen to him and even traces of everything that happens in the universe, even though God alone could recognize them all.[18]

---

16. An earlier draft of the following passage read: "Thus the circular shape of the ring of [Gyges] [Polycrates] does not contain everything that the notion of this particular ring contains, unlike God [knowing] seeing the individual notion of this ring [seeing, for example, that it will be swallowed by a fish and yet returned to its owner]." (Words in brackets were deleted by Leibniz.)

17. The word *haecceitas* (or *hecceïté*, what we are translating as "haecceity") was coined by John Duns Scotus (ca. 1270–1308) to refer to an individual essence or "thisness"— what *haecceitas* means literally.

18. An earlier draft added: "I speak here as if it were assumed that this ring [has consciousness] [is a substance]."

9. That Each Singular Substance Expresses the Whole Universe in Its Own Way, and That All Its Events, Together with All Their Circumstances and the Whole Sequence of External Things, Are Included in Its Notion.

SEVERAL notable paradoxes follow from this; among others, it follows that it is not true that two substances can resemble each other completely and differ only in number [*solo numero*],[19] and that what Saint Thomas asserts on this point about angels or intelligences (that here every individual is a lowest species)[20] is true of all substances, provided that one takes the specific difference as the geometers do with respect to their figures. It also follows that a substance can begin only by creation and end only by annihilation; that a substance is not divisible into two; that one substance cannot be constructed from two; and that thus the number of substances does not naturally increase and decrease, though they are often transformed.

Moreover, every substance is like a complete world and like a mirror of God or of the whole universe, which each one expresses in its own way, somewhat as the same city is variously represented depending upon the different positions from which it is viewed. Thus the universe is in some way multiplied as many times as there are substances, and the glory of God is likewise multiplied by as many entirely different representations of his work. It can even be said that every substance bears in some way the character of God's infinite wisdom and omnipotence and imitates him as much as it is capable. For it expresses, however confusedly, everything that happens in the universe, whether past, present, or future—this has some resemblance to an infinite perception or knowledge. And since all other substances in turn express this substance and accommodate themselves to it, one can say that it extends its power over all the others, in imitation of the creator's omnipotence.

10. That the Belief in Substantial Forms Has Some Basis, but That These Forms Do Not Change Anything in the Phenomena and Must Not Be Used to Explain Particular Effects.

IT SEEMS that the ancients, as well as many able men accustomed to deep meditation who have taught theology and philosophy some

---

19. An earlier draft added the following: "also, that if bodies are substances, it is not possible that their nature consists only in size, shape, and motion, but that something else is needed."

20. See St. Thomas, *Summa Theologiae* I, q. 50, art. 4.

centuries ago (some of whom are respected for their saintliness) have had some knowledge of what we have just said; this is why they introduced and maintained the substantial forms which are so decried today. But they are not so distant from the truth nor so ridiculous as the common lot of our new philosophers imagines.

I agree that the consideration of these forms serves no purpose in the details of physics and must not be used to explain particular phenomena. That is where the Scholastics failed, as did the physicians of the past who followed their example, believing that they could account for the properties of bodies by talking about forms and qualities without taking the trouble to examine their manner of operation. It is as if we were content to say that a clock has a quality of clockness derived from its form without considering in what all of this consists; that would be sufficient for the person who buys the clock, provided that he turns over its care to another.

But this misunderstanding and misuse of forms must not cause us to reject something whose knowledge is so necessary in metaphysics that, I hold, without it one cannot properly know the first principles or elevate our minds sufficiently well to the knowledge of incorporeal natures and the wonders of God.

However, just as a geometer does not need to burden his mind with the famous labyrinth of the composition of the continuum, there is no need for any moral philosopher and even less need for a jurist or statesman to trouble himself with the great difficulties involved in reconciling free will and God's providence, since the geometer can achieve all his demonstrations and the statesman can complete all his deliberations without entering into these discussions, discussions that remain necessary and important in philosophy and theology. In the same way, a physicist can explain some experiments, at times using previous simpler experiments and at times using geometric and mechanical demonstrations, without needing[21] general considerations from another sphere. And if he uses God's concourse, or else a soul, animating force [archée], or something else of this nature, he is raving just as much as the person who, in the course of an important practical deliberation, enters into a lofty discussion concerning the nature of destiny and the nature of our freedom. In fact, people often commit this fault without thinking when they encumber their minds with the consideration of fatalism and sometimes are even diverted from a good resolution or a necessary duty in this way.

---

21. An earlier draft continued "[forms and other] [considerations of substantial forms]".

11. That the Thoughts of the Theologians and Philosophers Who Are Called Scholastics Are Not Entirely to Be Disdained.

I KNOW that I am advancing a great paradox by attempting to rehabilitate the old philosophy in some fashion and to restore the almost banished substantial forms to their former place.[22] But perhaps I will not be condemned so easily when it is known that I have long meditated upon the modern philosophy, that I have given much time to experiments in physics and demonstrations in geometry, and that I had long been persuaded about the futility of these beings, which I finally was required to embrace in spite of myself and, as it were, by force, after having myself carried out certain studies. These studies made me recognize that our moderns do not give enough credit to Saint Thomas and to the other great men of his time and that there is much more solidity than one imagines in the opinions of the Scholastic philosophers and theologians, provided that they are used appropriately and in their proper place. I am even convinced that, if some exact and thoughtful mind took the trouble to clarify and summarize their thoughts after the manner of the analytic geometers, he would find there a great treasure of extremely important and wholly demonstrative truths.

12. That the Notions Involved in Extension Contain Something Imaginary and Cannot Constitute the Substance of Body.

BUT, to resume the thread of our discussion, I believe that anyone who will meditate about the nature of substance, as I have explained it above, will find[23] that the nature of body does not consist merely in extension, that is, in size, shape, and motion, but that we must necessarily recognize in body something related to souls, something we commonly call substantial form, even though it makes no change in the phenomena, any more than do the souls of animals, if they have any. It is even possible to demonstrate that the notions of size, shape, and motion are not as distinct as is imagined and that they contain something imaginary and relative to our perception, as do (though to a greater extent) color, heat, and other similar qualities,

---

22. A marginal note in an earlier draft: "I do this, however, only under an hypothesis, insofar as one can say that bodies are substances."
23. An earlier draft interpolates: "either that bodies are not substances in metaphysical rigor (which was, in fact, the view of the Platonists), or".

qualities about which one can doubt whether they are truly found in the nature of things outside ourselves. That is why qualities of this kind cannot constitute any substance. And if there were no other principle of identity in body other than the one just mentioned, a body could not subsist for more than a moment.

Yet the souls and substantial forms of other bodies are entirely different from intelligent souls, which alone know their actions. Not only don't intelligent souls perish naturally, but they also always preserve the basis for the knowledge of what they are; this is what renders them alone susceptible to punishment and reward and makes them citizens of the republic of the universe, whose monarch is God. It also follows that all other creatures must serve them—something which we will later discuss more fully.

13. Since the Individual Notion of Each Person Includes Once and for All Everything That Will Ever Happen to Him, One Sees in It the A Priori Proofs of the Truth of Each Event, or, Why One Happened Rather Than Another. But These Truths, However Certain, Are Nevertheless Contingent, Being Based on the Free Will of God or of His Creatures, Whose Choice Always Has Its Reasons, Which Incline without Necessitating.

BUT before going further, we must attempt to resolve a great difficulty that can arise from the foundations we have set forth above. We have said that the notion of an individual substance includes once and for all everything that can ever happen to it and that, by considering this notion, one can see there everything that can truly be said of it, just as we can see in the nature of a circle all the properties that can be deduced from it. But it seems that this would eliminate the difference between contingent and necessary truths, that there would be no place for human freedom, and that an absolute fatalism would rule all our actions as well as all the other events of the world. To this I reply that we must distinguish between what is certain and what is necessary. Everyone grants that future contingents are certain, since God foresees them, but we do not concede that they are necessary on that account. But (someone will say) if a conclusion can be deduced infallibly from a definition or notion, it is necessary. And it is true that we are maintaining that everything that must happen to a person is already contained virtually in his nature or notion, just as the properties of a circle are contained in its definition; thus the difficulty still remains. To address it firmly, I assert that connection or following [*consécution*] is of two kinds. The one whose contrary implies a contradiction is absolutely necessary; this deduction occurs in the eternal truths, for example, the truths of geometry. The other is necessary only *ex hypothesi* and, so to speak, accidentally, but it is contingent in itself, since its contrary does not imply a contradiction. And this connection is based not purely on ideas and God's simple understanding, but on his free decrees and on the sequence of the universe.

Let us take an example. Since Julius Caesar will become perpetual dictator and master of the republic and will overthrow the freedom of the Romans, this action is contained in his notion, for we assume that it is the nature of such a perfect notion of a subject to contain everything, so that the predicate is included in the subject, *ut possit inesse subjecto*.[24] It could be said that it is not in virtue of this notion or idea that he must perform this action, since it pertains to him only because God knows everything. But someone might insist that his nature or form corresponds to this notion, and, since God has imposed this personality on him, it is henceforth necessary for him to satisfy it. I could reply by citing future contingents, since they have no reality as yet, save in God's understanding and will, and, because God gave them this form in advance, they must in the same way correspond to it.

But I much prefer to overcome difficulties rather than to excuse them by giving some other similar difficulties, and what I am about to say will illuminate the one as well as the other. It is here, then, that we must apply the distinction concerning connections, and I say that whatever happens in conformity with these predeterminations [*avances*] is certain but not necessary, and if one were to do the contrary, he would not be doing something impossible in itself, even though it would be impossible [*ex hypothesi*] for this to happen. For if someone were able to carry out the whole demonstration by virtue of which he could prove this connection between the subject, Caesar, and the predicate, his successful undertaking, he would in fact be showing that Caesar's future dictatorship is grounded in his notion or nature, that there is a reason why he crossed the Rubicon rather than stopped at it and why he won rather than lost at Pharsalus and that it was reasonable, and consequently certain, that this should happen. But this would not show that it was necessary in itself nor

---

24. The Latin is an approximate paraphrase of the preceding clause.

that the contrary implies a contradiction. It is reasonable and certain in almost the same way that God will always do the best, even though what is less perfect does not imply a contradiction.

For it will be found that the demonstration of this predicate of Caesar is not as absolute as those of numbers or of geometry, but that it supposes the sequence of things that God has freely chosen, a sequence based on God's first free decree always to do what is most perfect and on God's decree with respect to human nature, following out of the first decree, that man will always do (although freely) that which appears to be best. But every truth based on these kinds of decrees is contingent, even though it is certain; for these decrees do not change the possibility of things, and, as I have already said, even though it is certain that God always chooses the best, this does not prevent something less perfect from being and remaining possible in itself, even though it will not happen, since it is not its impossibility but its imperfection which causes it to be rejected. And nothing is necessary whose contrary is possible.

We will therefore be in a position to satisfy these sorts of difficulties, however great they may appear (and in fact they are not made any the less pressing by considering the other thinkers who have ever treated this matter), as long as we recognize that all contingent propositions have reasons to be one way rather than another or else (what comes to the same thing) that they have *a priori* proofs of their truth which render them certain and which show that the connection between subject and predicate of these propositions has its basis in the natures of both. But they do not have necessary demonstrations, since these reasons are based only on the principle of contingency or the principle of the existence of things, that is, based on what is or appears to be best from among several equally possible things. On the other hand, necessary truths are based on the principle of contradiction and on the possibility or impossibility of essences themselves, without regard to the free will of God or his creatures.

14. God Produces Various Substances According to the Different Views He Has of the Universe, and through God's Intervention the Proper Nature of Each Substance Brings It about That What Happens to One Corresponds with What Happens to All the Others, without Their Acting upon One Another Directly.

AFTER having seen, in some way, what the nature of substances consists in, we must try to explain the dependence they have upon one another and their actions and passions. Now, first of all, it is very evident that created substances depend upon God, who preserves them and who even produces them continually by a kind of emanation, just as we produce our thoughts. For God, so to speak, turns on all sides and in all ways the general system of phenomena which he finds it good to produce in order to manifest his glory, and he views all the faces of the world in all ways possible, since there is no relation that escapes his omniscience. The result of each view of the universe, as seen from a certain position, is a substance which expresses the universe in conformity with this view, should God see fit to render his thought actual and to produce this substance. And since God's view is always true, our perceptions are always true; it is our judgments, which come from ourselves, that deceive us.

Now we said above, and it follows from what we have just said, that each substance is like a world apart, independent of all other things, except for God; thus all our phenomena, that is, all the things that can ever happen to us, are only consequences of our being. And since these phenomena maintain a certain order in conformity with our nature or, so to speak, in conformity with the world which is in us, an order which enables us to make useful observations to regulate our conduct, observations justified by the success of future phenomena, an order which thus allows us often to judge the future from the past without error, this would be sufficient to enable us to say that these phenomena are true without bothering with whether they are outside us and whether others also perceive them. Nevertheless, it is very true that the perceptions or expressions of all substances mutually correspond in such a way that each one, carefully following certain reasons or laws it has observed, coincides with others doing the same—in the same way that several people who have agreed to meet in some place at some specified time can really do this if they so desire. But although they all express the same phenomena, it does not follow that their expressions are perfectly similar; it is sufficient that they are proportional. In just the same way, several spectators believe that they are seeing the same thing and agree among themselves about it, even though each sees and speaks in accordance with his view.

And God alone (from whom all individuals emanate continually and who sees the universe not only as they see it but also entirely differently from all of them) is the cause of this correspondence of their phenomena and makes that which is particular to one of them public to all of them; otherwise, there would be no interconnection. We could therefore say in some way and properly speaking, though not in accordance with common usage, that one particular substance never acts upon another particular substance nor is acted upon by it, if we consider that what happens to each is solely a consequence of its complete idea or notion alone, since this idea already contains all its predicates or events and expresses the whole universe. In fact, nothing can happen to us except thoughts and perceptions, and all our future thoughts and perceptions are merely consequences, though contingent, of our preceding thoughts and perceptions, in such a way that, if I were capable of considering distinctly everything that happens or appears to me at this time, I could see in it everything that will ever happen or appear to me. This would never fail, and it would happen to me regardless, even if everything outside of me were destroyed, provided there remained only God and me. But since we attribute what we perceive in a certain way to other things as causes acting on us, we must consider the basis for this judgment and the element of truth there is in it.

15. The Action of One Finite Substance on Another Consists Only in the Increase of Degree of Its Expression Together with the Diminution of the Expression of the Other, Insofar as God Requires Them to Accommodate Themselves to One Another.

BUT, without entering into a long discussion, in order to reconcile the language of metaphysics with practice, it is sufficient for now to remark that we ascribe to ourselves—and with reason—the phenomena that we express most perfectly and that we attribute to other substances the phenomena that each expresses best. Thus a substance, which is of infinite extension insofar as it expresses everything, becomes limited in proportion to its more or less perfect manner of expression. This, then, is how one can conceive that substances impede or limit each other, and consequently one can say that, in this sense, they act upon one another and are required, so to speak, to accommodate themselves to one another. For it can happen that a change that increases the expression of one diminishes that of another. Now, the efficacy [vertu] a particular substance has is to express well the glory of God, and it is by doing this that it is less limited. And whenever something exercises its efficacy or power, that is, when it acts, it improves and extends itself insofar as it acts. Therefore, when a change takes place by which several substances are affected (in fact every change affects all of them), I believe one may say that the substance which immediately passes to a greater degree of perfection or to a more perfect expression exercises its power and *acts*, and the substance which passes to a lesser degree shows its weakness and *is acted upon* [*pâtit*]. I also hold that every action of a substance which has perception[25] involves some *pleasure*, and every passion some *pain* and vice versa. However, it can happen that a present advantage is destroyed by a greater evil in what follows, whence one can sin in acting, that is, in exercising one's power and finding pleasure.

16. God's Extraordinary Concourse Is Included in That Which Our Essence Expresses, for This Expression Extends to Everything. But This Concourse Surpasses the Powers of Our Nature or of Our Distinct Expression, Which Is Finite and Follows Certain Subordinate Maxims.

IT NOW only remains to explain how God can sometimes influence men and other substances by an extraordinary and miraculous concourse, since it seems that nothing extraordinary and supernatural can happen to them, given that all their events are only consequences of their nature. But we must remember what we have said above concerning miracles in the universe—that they are always in conformity with the universal law of the general order, even though they may be above the subordinate maxims. And to the extent that every person or substance is like a small world expressing the large world, we can say equally that the extraordinary action of God on this substance does not fail to be miraculous, despite the fact that it is included in the general order of the universe insofar as it is expressed by the essence or individual notion of this substance. That is why, if we include in our nature everything that it expresses, nothing is supernatural to it, for our nature extends everywhere, since an effect always expresses its cause and God is the true cause of substances. But what our nature expresses more perfectly belongs to it in a particular way, since it is in this that its power consists. But since it is limited, as I have just explained, there are many things that surpass the powers of our nature and even surpass the powers of all limited natures. Thus, to speak more clearly, I say that God's miracles and extraordinary concourse have the peculiarity that they cannot be foreseen by the reasoning of any created mind, no matter how enlightened, because the distinct comprehension of the general order sur-

---

25. The phrase "of a substance which has perception" was added in the margin.

passes all of them. On the other hand, everything that we call natural
depends on the less general maxims that creatures can understand.
Thus, in order that my words may be as irreproachable as my meaning, it would be good to connect certain ways of speaking with certain
thoughts. We could call that which includes everything we express
our essence or idea; since this expresses our union with God himself,
it has no limits and nothing surpasses it. But that which is limited in
us could be called our nature or our power; and in that sense, that
which surpasses the natures of all created substances is supernatural.

17. An Example of a Subordinate Maxim or Law of Nature; in Which It Is Shown, against the Cartesians and Many Others, That God Always Conserves the Same Force but Not the Same Quantity of Motion.

I HAVE already mentioned the subordinate maxims or laws of
nature often enough, and it seems appropriate to give an example of
one. Our new philosophers commonly make use of the famous rule
that God always conserves the same quantity of motion in the world.
In fact, this rule is extremely plausible, and, in the past, I held it as
indubitable. But I have since recognized what is wrong with it. It is
that Descartes and many other able mathematicians have believed
that the quantity of motion, that is, the speed multiplied by the size
of the moving body, coincides exactly with the moving force, or, to
speak geometrically, that the forces are proportional to the product
of the speeds and [sizes of] bodies. Now, it is extremely reasonable
that the same force is always conserved in the universe. Also, when we
attend to the phenomena, we see that there is no perpetual mechanical
motion, because then the force of a machine, which is always diminished somewhat by friction and which must sooner or later come to
an end, would restore itself, and consequently would increase by
itself without any new external impulsion. We observe also that the
force of a body is diminished only in proportion to the force it imparts
to some bodies contiguous to it or to its own parts, insofar as they
have separate motion.

Thus they believed that what can be said about force can also be
said about the quantity of motion. But to show the difference between
them, I assume that a body falling from a certain height acquires the
force to rise up that height, if its direction carries it that way, at least,
if there are no impediments. For example, a pendulum would rise
again exactly to the height from which it descended, if the resistance

of the air and some other small obstacles did not diminish its acquired force a little.

I assume also that as much force is required to elevate A, a body of one pound, to CD, a height of four fathoms, as to elevate B, a body of four pounds, to EF, a height of one fathom. All this is admitted by our new philosophers. It is therefore evident that, having fallen from height CD, body A acquired exactly as much force as did body B, which fell from height EF; for since body (B) reached F and acquired the force to rise to E (by the first assumption), it has the force to carry a body of four pounds, that is, itself, to EF, the height of one fathom; similarly, since body (A) reached D and acquired the force to rise to C, it has the force to carry a body of one pound, that is, itself, to CD, a height of four fathoms. Therefore (by the second assumption), the force of these two bodies is equal.

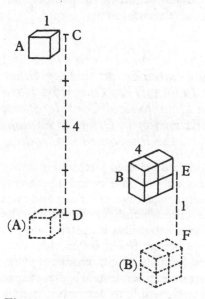

Figure 1

Let us now see whether the quantity of motion is also the same in each. But here we will be surprised to find a very great difference. For Galileo demonstrated that the speed acquired by the fall CD is twice the speed acquired by the fall EF, even though the one height is four times the other. Let us therefore multiply body A, proportional to 1, with its speed, proportional to 2; the product or quantity of motion will be proportional to 2. On the other hand, let us multiply body B, proportional to 4, by its speed, proportional to 1; the product or quantity of motion will be proportional to 4. Therefore the quantity of motion of body (A) at point D is half of the quantity of motion of body (B) at point F; yet their forces are equal. Hence, there is a great difference between quantity of motion and force—which is what needed to be proved.

Thus we see that force must be calculated from the quantity of the effect it can produce, for example, by the height to which a heavy

body of a certain size and kind can be raised; this is quite different
from the speed that can be imparted to it. And to give it double the
speed, it must be given more than double the force.

Nothing is simpler than this proof. Descartes fell into error here
only because he had too much confidence in his own thoughts, even
when they were not sufficiently ripe. But I am surprised that his
followers have not since then discovered this mistake; and I fear that
they are beginning, little by little, to imitate some of the Peripatetics,
whom they ridicule, like them gradually acquiring the habit of con-
sulting their master's writings rather than reason and nature.[26]

18. The Distinction between Force and Quantity of Motion Is Important, among Other Reasons, for Judging That One Must Have Recourse to Metaphysical Considerations Distinct from Extension in Order to Explain the Phenomena of Bodies.

THIS consideration, the distinction between force and quantity
of motion, is rather important, not only in physics and mechanics,
in order to find the true laws of nature and rules of motion and even
to correct the several errors of practice which have slipped into the
writings of some able mathematicians, but also in metaphysics, in
order to understand the principles better. For if we consider only
what motion contains precisely and formally, that is, change of place,
motion is not something entirely real, and when several bodies change
position among themselves, it is not possible to determine, merely
from a consideration of these changes, to which body we should
attribute motion or rest, as I could show geometrically, if I wished
to stop and do this now.

But the force or proximate cause of these changes is something
more real, and there is sufficient basis to attribute it to one body
more than to another. Also, it is only in this way that we can know
to which body the motion belongs. Now, this force is something

---

26. This section is a summary of an important paper Leibniz published in the *Acta
Eruditorum* on 6 January 1686, "A Brief Demonstration of a Notable Error of Descartes," translated in L 296–301, in which he argues against the conservation of
quantity of motion, size times speed, a law first framed by Descartes (*Principles of
Philosophy* II 36), and widely held by his followers. This essay began a long exchange
in the learned journals that came to be known as the *vis viva controversy*, over the
quantity, living force or *vis viva*, that Leibniz held was conserved. See "A Specimen
of Dynamics," part I, AG 117–130.

different from size, shape, and motion, and one can therefore judge that not everything conceived in body consists solely in extension and in its modifications, as our moderns have persuaded themselves. Thus we are once again obliged to reestablish some beings or forms they have banished. And it becomes more and more apparent that, although all the particular phenomena of nature can be explained mathematically or mechanically by those who understand them, nevertheless the general principles of corporeal nature and of mechanics itself are more metaphysical than geometrical, and belong to some indivisible forms or natures as the causes of appearances, rather than to corporeal mass or extension. This is a reflection capable of reconciling the mechanical philosophy of the moderns with the caution of some intelligent and well-intentioned persons who fear, with some reason, that we are withdrawing too far from immaterial beings, to the disadvantage of piety.

19. The Utility of Final Causes in Physics.

SINCE I do not like to judge people wrongly, I do not accuse our new philosophers, who claim to banish final causes from physics.[27] But I am nevertheless obliged to confess that the consequences of this opinion appear dangerous to me, especially if I combine it with the one I refuted at the beginning of this discourse, which seems to go so far as to eliminate final causes altogether, as if God proposed no end or good in acting or as if the good were not the object of his will. As for myself, I hold, on the contrary, that it is here we must seek the principle of all existences and laws of nature, because God always intends the best and most perfect.

I am quite willing to admit that we are subject to deception when we wish to determine God's ends or counsels. But this is only when we try to limit them to some particular design, believing that he had only one thing in view, when instead he regards everything at the same time. For instance, it is a great mistake to believe that God made the world only for us, although it is quite true that he made it in its entirety for us and that there is nothing in the universe which does not affect us and does not also accommodate itself in accordance with his regard for us, following the principles set forth above. Thus when we see some good effect or perfection occurring or ensuing

---

27. The "new philosophers" Leibniz has in mind include Descartes and Spinoza, who explain everything mechanically and reject final causes. See Descartes, *Principles of Philosophy* I 28, and the appendix to part I of Spinoza's *Ethics*. In an earlier draft, it is impiety that Leibniz is not accusing them of, but the phrase was deleted.

from God's works, we can say with certainty that God had proposed it. For he does nothing by chance and is not like us, who sometimes fail to do the good. That is why, far from being able to fall into error in this, as do extreme politicians who imagine too much subtlety in the designs of princes or as do commentators who look for too much erudition in their author, we cannot attribute too much reflection to this infinite wisdom, and there is no subject in which error is to be feared less, provided we limit ourselves to affirmations and avoid negative propositions that limit God's designs.

Anyone who sees the admirable structure of animals will find himself forced to recognize the wisdom of the author of things. And I advise those who have any feelings of piety and even feelings of true philosophy to keep away from the phrases of certain would-be freethinkers who say that we see because it happens that we have eyes and not that eyes were made for seeing. When one seriously holds these opinions ascribing everything to the necessity of matter or to some chance (even though both must appear ridiculous to those who understand what we have explained above), it is difficult to recognize an intelligent author of nature. For the effect must correspond to its cause; indeed, the effect is best recognized through a knowledge of the cause. Moreover, it is unreasonable to introduce a supreme intelligence as orderer of things and then, instead of using his wisdom, use only the properties of matter to explain the phenomena. This is as if, in order to account for the conquest of an important place by a great prince, a historian were to claim that it occurred because the small particles of gunpowder, set off by the contact of a spark, escaped with sufficient speed to push a hard and heavy body against the walls of the place, while the little particles that make up the brass of the cannon were so firmly interlaced that this speed did not separate them, instead of showing how the foresight of the conqueror enabled him to choose the suitable means and times and how his power overcame all obstacles.

20. A Noteworthy Passage by Socrates in Plato against the Philosophers Who Are Overly Materialistic.

THIS reminds me of a beautiful passage by Socrates in Plato's *Phaedo*. This passage agrees marvelously with my opinions on this point and seems to be directed expressly against our overly materialistic philosophers. Thus I have been tempted to translate this account, even though it is a little long; perhaps this sample will give an incentive to some of us to share in many of the other beautiful and solid thoughts which can be found in the writings of this famous author.[28]

21. If Mechanical Rules Depended Only on Geometry without Metaphysics, the Phenomena Would Be Entirely Different.

NOW, since we have always recognized God's wisdom in the detail of the mechanical structure of some particular bodies, it must also be displayed in the general economy of the world and in the constitution of the laws of nature. This is true to such an extent that one can observe the counsels of this wisdom in the laws of motion in general. For if there were nothing in bodies but extended mass and nothing in motion but change of place and if everything should and could be deduced solely from these definitions by geometrical necessity, it would follow, as I have shown elsewhere, that, upon contact, the smallest body would impart its own speed to the largest body without losing any of this speed; and we would have to accept a number of such rules which are completely contrary to the formation of a system.[29] But the decree of divine wisdom always to conserve the same total force and the same total direction has provided for this.

I even find that several effects of nature can be demonstrated doubly, that is, by considering first the efficient cause and then by considering the final cause, making use, for example, of God's decree always to produce his effect by the easiest and most determinate ways, as I have shown elsewhere in accounting for the rules of catoptrics and dioptrics;[30] I shall say more about this soon.

22. Reconciliation of Two Ways of Explaining Things, by Final Causes and by Efficient Causes, in Order to Satisfy Both Those Who Explain Nature Mechanically and Those Who Have Recourse to Incorporeal Natures.

IT IS appropriate to make this remark in order to reconcile those who hope to explain mechanically the formation of the first tissue of an animal and the whole machinery of its parts, with those who

---

28. Leibniz's marginal note: "The passage from Plato's *Phaedo* where Socrates ridicules Anaxagoras, who introduces mind but does not make use of it, is to be inserted." Leibniz repeats the passage in "Two Sects of Naturalists"; see AG 281–84.
29. See, e.g., AG 245–50 for the full argument.
30. The reference is to the "Unicum Opticae, Catoptricae et Dioptricae Principium, Autore G. G. L.," from the *Acta Eruditorum* (June 1682).

account for this same structure using final causes. Both ways are good and both can be useful, not only for admiring the skill of the Great Worker, but also for discovering something useful in physics and in medicine. And the authors who follow these different routes should not malign each other.

For I see that those who apply themselves to explaining the beauty of the divine anatomy laugh at others who imagine that a movement of certain fluids that seems fortuitous could have produced such a beautiful variety of limbs, and call these people rash and profane. And the latter, on the other hand, call the former simple and superstitious, comparing them to the ancients who regarded physicists as impious when they maintained that it is not Jupiter that thunders, but some matter present in the clouds. It would be best to join together both considerations, for if it is permitted to use a humble comparison, I recognize and praise the skill of a worker not only by showing his designs in making the parts of his machine, but also by explaining the instruments he used in making each part, especially when these instruments are simple and cleverly contrived. *And God is a skillful enough artisan* to produce a machine which is a thousand times more ingenious than that of our body, while using only some very simple fluids explicitly concocted in such a way that only the ordinary laws of nature are required to arrange them in the right way to produce so admirable an effect; but it is also true that this would not happen at all unless God were the author of nature.

However, I find that the way of efficient causes, which is in fact deeper and in some sense more immediate and *a priori*, is, on the other hand, quite difficult when one comes to details, and I believe that, for the most part, our philosophers are still far from it. But the way of final causes is easier, and is not infrequently of use in divining important and useful truths which one would be a long time in seeking by the other, more physical way; anatomy can provide significant examples of this. I also believe that Snell, who first discovered the rules of refraction, would have waited a long time before discovering them if he first had to find out how light is formed. But he apparently followed the method which the ancients used for catoptrics, which is in fact that of final causes. For, by seeking the easiest way to lead a ray from a given point to another point given by reflection on a given plane (assuming that this is nature's design), they discovered the equality of angles of incidence and angles of reflection, as can be seen in a little treatise by Heliodorus of Larissa, and elsewhere.[31] That is

31. Heliodorus of Larissa, or Damianos, was a Greek mathematician who flourished after Ptolemy. He was probably known to Leibniz through an edition, *De opticis libri duo*, published by Erasmus Bartholinus in Paris in 1657.

what, I believe, Snell and Fermat after him (though without knowing anything about Snell) have most ingeniously applied to refraction. For when, in the same media, rays observe the same proportion between sines (which is proportional to the resistances of the media), this happens to be the easiest or, at least, the most determinate way to pass from a given point in a medium to a given point in another. And the demonstration Descartes attempted to give of this same theorem by way of efficient causes is not nearly as good. At least there is room for suspicion that he would never have found the law in this way, if he had learned nothing in Holland of Snell's discovery.[32]

23. To Return to Immaterial Substances, We Explain How God Acts on the Understanding of Minds and Whether We Always Have the Idea of That About Which We Think.

I found it appropriate to insist a bit on these considerations of final causes, incorporeal natures, and an intelligent cause with respect to bodies, in order to show their use even in physics and mathematics: on the one hand, to purge the mechanical philosophy of the impiety with which it is charged and, on the other hand, to elevate the minds of our philosophers from material considerations alone to nobler meditations. It is now appropriate to return from bodies to immaterial natures, in particular to minds, and to say something of the means God uses to enlighten them and act on them. In this matter, too, we must not doubt that there are certain laws of nature, of which I could speak more fully elsewhere. But for now it will be sufficient to touch somewhat on ideas, whether we see all things in God and how God is our light.[33]

It may be appropriate to observe that the improper use of ideas gives rise to several errors. For when we reason about something, we imagine ourselves to have the idea of that thing; and that is the foundation upon which certain ancient and new philosophers have built a certain extremely imperfect demonstration of God. For, they say, I must have an idea of God or of a perfect being since I think of him, and one cannot think without an idea. Now, the idea of this

---

32. The law of refraction was first published in the second discourse of Descartes's *Dioptrics*. Descartes does indeed attempt to derive the law from hypotheses about the nature of light (see Ols, pp. 75–83). Snell discovered the same laws at roughly the same time as Descartes, and there was (and continues to be) a lively dispute about who discovered the law first, and whether Descartes actually discovered the law or learned it from Snell. Leibniz seems to favor Snell.

33. See Malebranche, *Search after Truth*, book III, pt. 2, chap. 6.

being contains all perfections, and existence is a perfection, so consequently he exists. But since we often think of impossible chimeras—for example, of the highest degree of speed, of the greatest number, of the intersection of the conchoid with its base or rule—this reasoning is insufficient. It is therefore in this sense that we can say that there are true and false ideas, depending upon whether the thing in question is possible or not. And it is only when we are certain of its possibility that we can boast of having an idea of the thing. Thus the argument above proves, at least, that God exists necessarily, if he is possible. It is indeed a prerogative of divine nature, one that surpasses all others, that divine nature needs only its possibility or essence in order actually to exist, and it is precisely this that is called *ens a se*.

24. What Is Clear or Obscure, Distinct or Confused, Adequate and Intuitive or Suppositive[34] Knowledge; Nominal, Real, Causal, and Essential Definition.

IN ORDER to understand better the nature of ideas, we must to some extent touch on the varieties of knowledge. When I can recognize a thing from among others without being able to say what its differences or properties consist in, the knowledge is *confused*. It is in this way that we sometimes know something *clearly*, without being in any doubt whether a poem or a picture is done well or badly, simply because it has a certain something, I know not what, that satisfies or offends us. But when I can explain the marks which I have, the knowledge is called *distinct*. And such is the knowledge of an assayer, who discerns the true from the false by means of certain tests or marks which make up the definition of gold.

But distinct knowledge has degrees, for ordinarily the notions that enter into the definition would themselves need definition and are known only confusedly. But when everything that enters into a distinct definition or distinct knowledge is known distinctly, down to the primitive notions, I call this knowledge *adequate*. And when my mind understands all the primitive ingredients of a notion at once and distinctly, it has *intuitive* knowledge of it; this is extremely rare, since the greater part of human knowledge is only confused or *suppositive*.[35]

---

34. Cf. "Meditations on Knowledge, Truth, and Ideas" (1684), AG 23–27. Instead of 'suppositive' Leibniz there uses the term 'symbolic'.
35. In the margin: "A notion intermediate between intuitive and clear is when I have been deprived of clear knowledge of all surrounding notions."

It is also good to distinguish nominal and real definitions. I call a definition *nominal* when one can still doubt whether the notion defined is possible, as, for example, if I say that an endless helix is a solid line whose parts are congruent or can be superimposed on one another; anyone who does not know from elsewhere what an endless helix is could doubt whether such a line is possible, even though having such congruent parts is in fact one of the reciprocal properties of the endless helix, for other lines whose parts are congruent (which are only the circumference of a circle and the straight line) are planar, that is, they can be inscribed on a plane. This shows that any reciprocal property can serve as a nominal definition; but when the property makes known the possibility of the thing, it constitutes a real definition. As long as we have only a nominal definition, we cannot be certain of the consequences we derive, for if it concealed some contradiction or impossibility, the opposite conclusions could be derived from it. That is why truths do not depend upon names and are not arbitrary, as some new philosophers have believed.[36]

Furthermore, there are still great differences between the kinds of real definitions. For when possibility is proved only by experience, as in the definition of quicksilver, whose possibility we know because we know that there actually is such a body which is an extremely heavy but rather volatile fluid, the definition is merely real and nothing more; but when the proof of the possibility is a *priori*, the definition is both real and *causal*, as when it contains the possible generation of the thing. And when a definition pushes the analysis back to the primitive notions without assuming anything requiring an *a priori* proof of its possibility, it is perfect or *essential*.

25. *In What Case Our Knowledge Is Joined to the Contemplation of the Idea.*

NOW, it is evident that we have no idea of a notion when it is impossible. And in the case where knowledge is only *suppositive*, even when we have the idea, we do not contemplate it, for such a notion is only known in the way in which we know notions involving a hidden impossibility [*occultement impossibles*]; and if a notion is possible, we do not learn its possibility in this way. For example, when I think of a thousand or of a chiliagon, I often do this without contemplating the idea—as when I say that a thousand is ten times a hundred

---

36. Leibniz probably has Hobbes in mind here. See the "Dialogue" (August 1677), AG 268–72.

without bothering to think of what 10 and 100 are because I *suppose* I know it and do not believe I need to stop now and conceive it. Thus, it could happen, as in fact it often happens, that I am mistaken with respect to a notion I suppose or believe that I understand, although in fact the notion is impossible, or at least incompatible with those to which I join it. And whether I am mistaken or not, this suppositive way of conceiving remains the same. Therefore, only in confused notions when our knowledge is *clear* or in distinct notions when it is *intuitive* do we see the entire idea in them.[37]

26. That We Have All Ideas in Us; and of Plato's Doctrine of Reminiscence.

IN ORDER properly to conceive what an idea is, we must prevent an equivocation. For some take the idea to be the form or difference of our thoughts, and thus we have an idea in the mind only insofar as we think of it; every time we think of it again, we have other ideas of the same thing, though similar to the preceding ideas. But it seems that others take the idea as an immediate object of thought or as some permanent form that remains when we are not contemplating it. And, in fact, our soul always has in it the quality of representing to itself any nature or form whatsoever, when the occasion to think of it presents itself. And I believe that this quality of our soul, insofar as it expresses some nature, form, or essence, is properly the idea of the thing, which is in us and which is always in us, whether we think of it or not. For our soul expresses God, the universe, and all essences, as well as all existences.

This agrees with my principles, for nothing ever enters into our mind naturally from the outside; and we have a bad habit of thinking of our soul as if it received certain species as messengers and as if it has doors and windows. We have all these forms in our mind; we even have forms from all time, for the mind always expresses all its future thoughts and already thinks confusedly about everything it will ever think about distinctly. And nothing can be taught to us whose idea we do not already have in our mind, an idea which is like the matter of which that thought is formed.

This is what Plato so excellently recognized when he proposed his doctrine of reminiscence, a very solid doctrine, provided that it is taken rightly and purged of the error of preexistence and provided

---

37. An earlier draft continues: "However, we actually have in our mind all possible ideas, and we always think of them in a confused way."

that we do not imagine that at some earlier time the soul must already have known and thought distinctly what it learns and thinks now. Plato also strengthened his view by way of a fine experiment, introducing a little boy, whom he leads insensibly to extremely difficult truths of geometry concerning incommensurables without teaching him anything, merely by asking appropriate questions in proper order.[38] This demonstrates that our soul knows all these things virtually and requires only *attention* to recognize truths, and that, consequently, it has, at very least, the ideas upon which these truths depend. One can even say that it already possesses these truths, if they are taken as relations of ideas.

27. How Our Soul Can Be Compared to Empty Tablets and How Our Notions Come from the Senses.

ARISTOTLE preferred to compare our soul to tablets that are still blank, where there is room for writing,[39] and he maintained that nothing is in our understanding that does not come from the senses. That agrees better with the popular notions, as is Aristotle's way, but Plato goes deeper. However, these kinds of doxologies or practicologies may be acceptable in ordinary usage, much as we see that those who follow Copernicus do not stop saying that the sun rises and sets. I even find that they can be given a good sense, a sense according to which they have nothing false in them, just as I have already noted how one can truly say that particular substances act on one another. In this same way, one can also say that we receive knowledge from the outside by way of the senses, because some external things contain or express more particularly the reasons that determine our soul to certain thoughts. But when we are concerned with the exactness of metaphysical truths, it is important to recognize the extent and independence of our soul, which goes infinitely further than is commonly thought, though in ordinary usage in life we attribute to it only what we perceive most manifestly and what belongs to us most particularly, for it serves no purpose to go any further.

---

38. This is a reference to Plato's *Meno*, 82b *et seq.*, where, in a familiar passage, Socrates leads a young slave boy through some geometrical arguments.
39. Aristotle, *De Anima*, Book II, chap. 4. The doctrine that nothing is in the intellect that was not first in the senses, attributed to Aristotle by the Scholastics, does not actually occur in Aristotle; perhaps it is a rendering of *Posterior Analytics*, Book II, chap. 19, or *Nicomachean Ethics*, Book VI, chap. 3, sec. 3.

However, it would be good to choose terms proper to each conception [sens] in order to avoid equivocation. Thus, the expressions in our soul, whether we conceive them or not, can be called *ideas*, but those we conceive or form can be called *notions, concepts* [*conceptus*]. But however we take these expressions, it is always false to say that all our notions come from the external senses, for the notions I have of myself and of my thoughts, and consequently of being, substance, action, identity, and of many others, arise from an internal experience.

28. God Alone Is the Immediate Object of Our Perceptions, Which Exist Outside of Us, and He Alone Is Our Light.

NOW, in rigorous metaphysical truth, there is no external cause acting on us except God alone, and he alone communicates himself to us immediately in virtue of our continual dependence. From this it follows that there is no other external object that touches our soul and immediately excites our perception. Thus we have ideas of everything in our soul only by virtue of God's continual action on us, that is to say, because every effect expresses its cause, and thus the essence of our soul is a certain expression, imitation or image of the divine essence, thought, and will, and of all the ideas comprised in it. It can then be said that God is our immediate external object and that we see all things by him. For example, when we see the sun and the stars, it is God who has given them to us and who conserves the ideas of them in us, and it is God who determines us really to think of them by his ordinary concourse while our senses are disposed in a certain manner, according to the laws he has established. God is the sun and the light of souls, the light that lights every man that comes into this world,[40] and this is not an opinion new to our times. After Holy Scripture and the Church Fathers, who have always preferred Plato to Aristotle, I remember having previously noted that from the time of the Scholastics, several believed that God is the light of the soul and, in their way of speaking, the active intellect of the rational soul. The Averroists gave the sense of this a bad turn,[41] but others, among whom was, I believe, William of St. Amour, and

---

40. John 1:9.
41. Averroists were Christian followers of Averroes (or Ibn Rushd—1126–98), the great Arabic commentator on Aristotle, who held that the active intellect in each man is part of a single active intellect. The doctrine of a single world-soul was condemned as heresy.

several mystical theologians, have taken it in a manner worthy of God and capable of elevating the soul to the knowledge of its good.

29. Yet We Think Immediately through Our Own Ideas and Not through Those of God.

HOWEVER, I am not of the opinion of certain able philosophers who seem to maintain that our very ideas are in God and not at all in us.[42] In my opinion, this arises from the fact that they have not yet considered sufficiently either what we have just explained about substances or the full extent and independence of our soul, which makes it contain everything that happens to it, and makes it express God and, with him, all possible and actual beings, just as an effect expresses its cause. Also, it is inconceivable that I think through the ideas of others. The soul must actually be affected in a certain way when it thinks of something, and it must already have in itself not only the passive power of being able to be affected in this way (which is already wholly determined) but also an active power, a power by virtue of which there have always been in its nature marks of the future production of this thought and dispositions to produce it in its proper time. And all this already involves the idea included in this thought.

30. How God Inclines Our Soul without Necessitating It; That We Do Not Have the Right to Complain and That We Must Not Ask Why Judas Sins but Only Why Judas the Sinner Is Admitted to Existence in Preference to Some Other Possible Persons. On Original Imperfection before Sin and on the Degrees of Grace.

THERE ARE a number of considerations with respect to the action of God on human will which are so difficult that it would be inordinately lengthy to pursue them here. Roughly speaking, however, here is what can be said. In concurring with our actions, God ordinarily does no more than follow the laws he has established, that is, he continually conserves and produces our being in such a way that thoughts come to us spontaneously or freely in the order that the notion pertaining to our individual substance contains them,

---

42. Malebranche, again, is Leibniz's primary target, as above in sec. 23.

a notion in which they could be foreseen from all eternity. Moreover, in virtue of his decree that the will always tend toward the apparent good, expressing or imitating his will in certain particular respects (so that this apparent good always has some truth in it), God determines our will to choose what seems better, without, however, necessitating it. For, absolutely speaking, the will is in a state of indifference, as opposed to one of necessity, and it has the power to do otherwise or even to suspend its action completely; these two alternatives are possible and remain so.

Therefore the soul must guard itself against deceptive appearances [les surprises des apparences] through a firm will to reflect and neither to act nor to judge in certain circumstances except after having deliberated fully. But it is true, and it is even assured from all eternity, that a certain soul will not make use of this power in such a situation. But who is to blame? Can the soul complain about anything other than itself? All these complaints after the fact are unjust, if they would have been unjust before the fact. Now, could this soul, a little before sinning, complain about God in good faith, as if God determined it to sin? Since God's determinations in these matters cannot be foreseen, how does the soul know that it is determined to sin, unless it is actually sinning already? It is only a matter of not willing, and God could not put forth an easier and more just condition; thus judges do not seek the reasons which have disposed a man to have a bad will, but only stop to consider the extent to which this particular will is bad. But perhaps it is certain from all eternity that I shall sin? Answer this question for yourself: perhaps not; and without considering what you cannot know and what can give you no light, act according to your duty, which you do know.

But someone else will say, why is it that this man will assuredly commit this sin? The reply is easy: otherwise it would not be this man. For God sees from all time that there will be a certain Judas whose notion or idea (which God has) contains this free and future action. Therefore only this question remains, why does such a Judas, the traitor, who is merely possible in God's idea, actually exist? But no reply to this question is to be expected on earth, except that, in general, one must say that, since God found it good that he should exist, despite the sin that God foresaw, it must be that this sin is paid back with interest in the universe, that God will derive a greater good from it, and that it will be found that, in sum, the sequence of things in which the existence of that sinner is included is the most perfect among all the possible sequences. But we cannot always explain the admirable economy of this choice while we are travellers in this world;

it is enough to know it without understanding it. And here is the occasion to recognize the *altitudinem divitarum*, the depth and abyss of divine wisdom, without seeking a detail that involves infinite considerations.[43]

Yet one sees clearly that God is not the cause of evil. For not only did original sin take possession of the soul after the innocence of men had been lost, but even before this, there was an original imperfection or limitation connatural to all creatures, which makes them liable to sin or capable of error. Thus, the supralapsarians[44] raise no more problems than the others do. And it is to this, in my view, that we must reduce the opinion of Saint Augustine and other authors, the opinion that the root of evil is in nothingness, that is to say, in the privation or limitation of creatures, which God graciously remedies by the degree of perfection it pleases him to give. This grace of God, whether ordinary or extraordinary, has its degrees and its measures; in itself, it is always efficacious in producing a certain proportionate effect, and, further, it is always sufficient, not only to secure us from sin, but even to produce salvation, assuming that man unites himself to it by what derives from him.[45] But it is not always sufficient to overcome man's inclinations, for otherwise he would have nothing more to strive for; this is reserved solely for the absolutely efficacious grace which is always victorious, whether it is so by itself or by way of appropriate circumstances.

31. On the Motives of Election, on Faith Foreseen, on Middle Knowledge, on the Absolute Decree and That It All Reduces to the Reason Why God Has Chosen for Existence Such a Possible Person Whose Notion Includes Just Such a Sequence of Graces and Free Acts; This Puts an End to All Difficulties at Once.

FINALLY, God's graces are wholly pure graces, upon which creatures have no claim. However, just as it is not sufficient to appeal to God's absolute or conditional foresight into the future actions of men in order to account for his choice in the dispensation of these graces, we also must not imagine absolute decrees that have no reasonable motive. As for God's foreknowledge of faith or good

---

43. The Latin translates: "depth of riches," a reference to Romans 11:33.
44. Calvinists who held that God's decrees of election and reprobation preceded the fall. Cf. *Theodicy* I, sec. 77–84.
45. The text also contains "by his will" as a possible ending for the sentence.

works, it is very true that he has elected only those whose faith and charity he foresaw, whom he foreknew he would endow with faith. But the same question returns, why will God give the grace of faith or of good works to some rather than to others? And as for this knowledge God has, which is the foresight not of faith and good works, but of their grounds [*matière*] and predisposition, that is, foresight of what a man would contribute to them on his side (for it is true that there are differences among men whenever there are differences in grace and that, in fact, although a man needs to be stimulated to the good and be converted, he must also act in that direction afterward), it seems to several people that one could say that God, seeing what a man would do without grace or extraordinary assistance, or at least seeing the sort of person he is, leaving grace aside, might resolve to give grace to those whose natural dispositions were better or, at least, less imperfect or less bad. But even if that were the case, one can say that these natural dispositions, insofar as they are good, are still the effect of grace, although ordinary grace, since God has favored some more than others. And since he knows that these natural advantages he gives will serve as motives for grace or extraordinary assistance, is it not true, according to this doctrine, that in the end everything is completely reduced to his mercy?

Since we do not know how much and in what way God takes account of natural dispositions in the dispensation of grace, I believe, then, that the most exact and surest thing to say, according to our principles, as I have already noted, is that among the possible beings there must be the person of Peter or John, whose notion or idea contains this entire sequence of ordinary and extraordinary graces and all the rest of these events with their circumstances, and that it pleased God to choose him for actual existence from among an infinity of equally possible persons. After this it seems that there is nothing more to ask and that all difficulties vanish.

For, with respect to this single great question, why it pleased God to choose him from among so many other possible persons, one would have to be very unreasonable not to be content with the general reasons we have given, reasons whose details lie beyond us. Thus, instead of having recourse to an absolute decree which is unreasonable, since it is without reason, or to reasons which do not solve the difficulty completely and are in need of further reasons, it would be best to say with Saint Paul, that God here followed certain great reasons of wisdom or appropriateness, unknown to mortals and based on the general order, whose aim is the greatest perfection of the universe. It is to this that the motives of the glory of God and the manifestation of his justice are reduced, as well as of his mercy and generally of his perfections and finally the immense depth of his riches, with which the soul of Saint Paul was enraptured.

32. The Utility of These Principles in Matters of Piety and Religion.

FOR THE REST, it seems that the thoughts we have just explained, particularly the great principle of the perfection of the operations of God and the principle that the notion of a substance contains all its events with all their circumstances, far from harming, serve to confirm religion, to dispel enormous difficulties, to enflame souls with a divine love, and to elevate minds to the knowledge of incorporeal substances, much more than hypotheses we have seen until now. For one sees clearly that all other substances depend on God, in the same way as thoughts emanate from our substance, that God is all in all, and that he is intimately united with all creatures, in proportion to their perfection, that it is he alone who determines them from the outside by his influence, and, if to act is to determine immediately, it can be said in this sense, in the language of metaphysics, that God alone operates on me, and God alone can do good or evil to me; the other substances contribute only by reason of these determinations, because God, having regard for all, shares his blessings and requires them to accommodate themselves to one another. Hence God alone brings about the connection and communication among substances, and it is through him that the phenomena of any substance meet and agree with those of others and consequently, that there is reality in our perceptions. But, in practice, one ascribes an action to particular reasons[46] in the sense that I have explained above, because it is not necessary always to mention the universal cause in particular cases.

We also see that every substance has a perfect spontaneity (which becomes freedom in intelligent substances), that everything that happens to it is a consequence of its idea or of its being, and that nothing determines it, except God alone. And that is why a person of very exalted mind, revered for her saintliness, was in the habit of saying that the soul must often think as if there were nothing but God and itself in the world.[47]

---

46. An earlier draft had "occasional causes" rather than "particular reasons".
47. Leibniz probably had St. Theresa in mind here. In a letter from 1696 he wrote: "In [her writings] I once found this lovely thought, that the soul should conceive of things as if there were only God and itself in the world. This even provides a considerable object to reflect upon in philosophy, which I usefully employed in one of my hypotheses" (Gr. 103).

Now, nothing gives us a stronger understanding of immortality than the independence and extent of the soul in question here, which shelters it absolutely from all external things, since the soul alone makes up its whole world and is sufficient to itself with God. And it is as impossible that it should perish without annihilation, as it is that the world (of which it is a perpetual living expression) should destroy itself; hence, it is impossible that the changes in this extended mass called our body should do anything to the soul or that the dissolution of this body should destroy what is indivisible.

33. Explanation of the Union of Soul and Body, a Matter Which Has Been Considered as Inexplicable or Miraculous, and on the Origin of Confused Perceptions.

WE ALSO see the unexpected illumination of this great mystery of the union of the soul and the body, that is, how it happens that the passions and actions of the one are accompanied by the actions and passions, or by the corresponding phenomena, of the other. For there is no way to conceive that the one has any influence on the other, and it is unreasonable simply to appeal to the extraordinary operation of the universal cause in an ordinary and particular thing. But here is the true reason: we have said that everything that happens to the soul and to each substance follows from its notion, and therefore the very idea or essence of the soul carries with it the fact that all its appearances or perceptions must arise spontaneously from its own nature and precisely in such a way that they correspond by themselves to what happens in the whole universe. But they correspond more particularly and more perfectly to what happens in the body assigned to it, because the soul expresses the state of the universe in some way and for some time, according to the relation other bodies have to its own body. This also allows us to know how our body belongs to us, without, however, being attached to our essence. And I believe that persons who can meditate will judge our principles favorably, because they will be able to see easily what the connection between the soul and the body consists in, a connection which seems inexplicable in any other way.

We also see that the perceptions of our senses, even when they are clear, must necessarily contain some confused feeling [sentiment], for our body receives the impression of all other bodies, since all the bodies of the universe are in sympathy, and, even though our senses are related to everything, it is impossible for our soul to attend to everything in particular; that is why our confused sensations are the result of a truly infinite variety of perceptions. This is almost like the confused murmur coming from the innumerable set of breaking waves heard by those who approach the seashore. Now, if from several perceptions (which do not come together to make one), there is none which stands out before the others and if they make impressions that are almost equally strong or equally capable of gaining the attention of the soul, the soul can only perceive them confusedly.

34. On the Difference between Minds and Other Substances, Souls or Substantial Forms, and That the Immortality Required Includes Memory.

ASSUMING[48] that the bodies that make up an *unum per se*, as does man, are substances, that they have substantial forms, and that animals have souls, we must admit that these souls and these substantial forms cannot entirely perish, no more than atoms or the ultimate parts of matter can, on the view of other philosophers. For no substance perishes, although it can become completely different. They also express the whole universe, although more imperfectly than minds do. But the principal difference is that they do not know what they are nor what they do, and consequently, since they do not reflect on themselves, they cannot discover necessary and universal truths. It is also because they lack reflection about themselves that they have no moral qualities. As a result, though they may pass through a thousand transformations, like those we see when a caterpillar changes into a butterfly, yet from the moral or practical point of view, the result is as if they had perished; indeed, we may even say that they have perished physically, in the sense in which we say that bodies perish through their corruption. But the intelligent soul, knowing what it is—having the ability to utter the word "I," a word so full of meaning—does not merely remain and subsist metaphysically, which it does to a greater degree than the others, but also remains the same morally and constitutes the same person. For it is memory or the knowledge of this self that renders it capable of punishment or reward. Thus the immortality required in morality and religion does not consist merely in this perpetual subsistence common to all

---

48. An earlier draft began with this first sentence: "I do not attempt to determine if bodies are substances in metaphysical rigor or if they are only *true* phenomena like the rainbow and, consequently, if there are true substances, souls, or substantial forms which are not intelligent."

substances, for without the memory of what one has been, there would be nothing desirable about it. Suppose that some person all of a sudden becomes the king of China, but only on the condition that he forgets what he has been, as if he were born anew; practically, or as far as the effects could be perceived, wouldn't that be the same as if he were annihilated and a king of China created at the same instant in his place? That is something this individual would have no reason to desire.

35. The Excellence of Minds and That God Considers Them Preferable to Other Creatures. That Minds Express God Rather Than the World, but That the Other Substances Express the World Rather Than God.

BUT SO THAT we may judge by natural reasons that God will always preserve not only our substance, but also our person, that is, the memory and knowledge of what we are (though distinct knowledge is sometimes suspended during sleep and fainting spells), we must join morals to metaphysics, that is, we must not only consider God as the principle and cause of all substances and all beings, but also as the leader of all persons or intelligent substances and as the absolute monarch of the most perfect city or republic, which is what the universe composed of all minds together is, God himself being the most perfect of all minds and the greatest of all beings. For certainly minds are the most perfect beings[49] and best express divinity. And since the whole nature, end, virtue, and function of substance is merely to express God and the universe, as has been sufficiently explained, there is no reason to doubt that the substances which express the universe with the knowledge of what they are doing and which are capable of knowing great truths about God and the universe, express it incomparably better than do those natures, which are either brutish and incapable of knowing truths or completely destitute of sensation and knowledge. And the difference between intelligent substances and substances that have no intelligence at all is just as great as the difference between a mirror and someone who sees.

Since God himself is the greatest and wisest of all minds, it is easy to judge that the beings with whom he can, so to speak, enter into

---

49. An earlier draft of this sentence began: ". . . minds are either the only substances one finds in the world, in the case in which bodies are only true phenomena, or else they are at least the most perfect . . ."

conversation, and even into a society—by communicating to them his views and will in a particular manner and in such a way that they can know and love their benefactor—must be infinitely nearer to him than all other things, which can only pass for the instruments of minds. So we see that all wise persons value a man infinitely more than any other thing, no matter how precious it is, and it seems that the greatest satisfaction that a soul, content in other ways, can have is to see itself loved by others. With respect to God, though, there is the difference that his glory and our worship cannot add anything to his satisfaction, since knowledge of creatures is only a consequence of his supreme and perfect happiness—far from contributing to it or being its partial cause. However, what is good and reasonable in finite minds is found preeminently in him, and, just as we would praise a king who would prefer to preserve the life of a man rather than the most precious and rarest of his animals, we should not doubt that the most enlightened and most just of all monarchs is of the same opinion.

36. God Is the Monarch of the Most Perfect Republic, Composed of All Minds, and the Happiness of This City of God Is His Principal Purpose.

INDEED, minds are the most perfectible substances, and their perfections are peculiar in that they interfere with each other the least, or rather they aid one another the most, for only the most virtuous can be the most perfect friends. Whence it obviously follows that God, who always aims for the greatest perfection in general, will pay the greatest attention to minds and will give them the greatest perfection that universal harmony can allow, not only in general, but to each of them in particular.

One can even say that God, insofar as he is a mind, is the originator of existences; otherwise, if he lacked the will to choose the best, there would be no reason for a possible thing to exist in preference to others. Thus the quality that God has of being a mind himself takes precedence over all the other considerations he can have toward creatures; only minds are made in his image and are, as it were, of his race or like children of his household, since they alone can serve him freely and act with knowledge in imitation of the divine nature; a single mind is worth a whole world, since it does not merely express the world but it also knows it and it governs itself after the fashion of God. In this way we may say that, although all substances express the whole universe, nevertheless the other substances express the world rather than God, while minds express God rather than the world. And this nature of minds, so noble that it brings them as near to divinity as it is possible for simple creatures, has the result that God draws infinitely more glory from them than from all other beings, or rather the other beings only furnish minds the matter for glorifying him.

That is why this moral quality God has, which makes him the lord or monarch of minds, relates to him, so to speak, personally and in a quite singular manner. It is because of this that he humanizes himself, that he is willing to allow anthropomorphism, and that he enters into society with us, as a prince with his subjects; and this consideration is so dear to him that the happy and flourishing state of his empire, which consists in the greatest possible happiness of its inhabitants, becomes the highest of his laws. For happiness is to people what perfection is to beings. And if the first principle of the existence of the physical world is the decree to give it the greatest perfection possible, the first intent of the moral world or the City of God, which is the noblest part of the universe, must be to diffuse in it the greatest possible happiness.

Therefore we must not doubt that God has ordered everything in such a way that minds not only may live always, which is certain, but also that they may always preserve their moral quality, so that the city does not lose a single person, just as the world does not lose any substance. And consequently they will always know what they are, otherwise they would not be susceptible to reward or punishment, something, however, essential to a republic, but above all essential to the most perfect republic, in which nothing can be neglected.

Finally, since God is at the same time the most just and most good-natured of monarchs and since he demands only a good will, as long as it is sincere and serious, his subjects cannot wish for a better condition, and, to make them perfectly happy, he wants only for them to love him.

37. *Jesus Christ Has Revealed to Men the Mystery and Admirable Laws of the Kingdom of Heaven and the Greatness of the Supreme Happiness That God Prepares for Those Who Love Him.*

T HE ANCIENT philosophers knew very little of these important truths; Jesus Christ alone has expressed them divinely well and in a manner so clear and familiar that the coarsest of minds have grasped them. Thus his gospel has entirely changed the course of human affairs; he has brought us to know the kingdom of heaven, or that perfect republic of minds which deserves the title of City of God, whose admirable laws he has disclosed to us. He alone has made us see how much God loves us and with what exactitude he has provided for everything that concerns us; that, caring for sparrows, he will not neglect the rational beings which are infinitely more dear to him; that all the hairs on our head are numbered; that heaven and earth will perish rather than the word of God and what pertains to the economy of our salvation; that God has more regard for the least of the intelligent souls than for the whole machinery of the world; that we must not fear those who can destroy bodies but cannot harm souls, because God alone can make souls happy or unhappy; and that the souls of the just, in his hands, are safe from all the upheavals of the universe, God alone being able to act upon them; that none of our actions are forgotten; that everything is taken account of, even idle words or a spoonful of water well used; finally, that everything must result in the greatest welfare of those who are good; that the just will be like suns; and that neither our senses nor our mind has ever tasted anything approaching the happiness that God prepares for those who love him.

On the Ultimate Origination of Things (23 November 1697)[50]

BEYOND THE WORLD, that is, beyond the collection of finite things, there is some One Being who rules, not only as the soul is the ruler in me, or, better, as the self is the ruler in my body, but also in a much higher sense. For the One Being who rules the universe not only rules the world, but also fashions or creates it; he is above the world, and, so to speak, extramundane, and therefore he is the ultimate reason for things. For we cannot find in any of the individual things, or even in the entire collection and series of things, a sufficient reason for why they exist. Let us suppose that a book on the elements of geometry has always existed, one copy always made from another. It is obvious that although we can explain a present copy of the book from the previous book from which it was copied, this will never lead

---

50. G VII 302–8. Latin.

us to a complete explanation, no matter how many books back we go, since we can always wonder why there have always been such books, why these books were written, and why they were written the way they were. What is true of these books is also true of the different states of the world, for the state which follows is, in a sense, copied from the preceding state, though in accordance with certain laws of change. And so, however far back we might go into previous states, we will never find in those states a complete explanation [ratio] for why, indeed, there is any world at all, and why it is the way it is.

I certainly grant that you can imagine that the world is eternal. However, since you assume only a succession of states, and since no reason for the world can be found in any one of them whatsoever (indeed, assuming as many of them as you like won't in any way help you to find a reason), it is obvious that the reason must be found elsewhere. For in eternal things, even if there is no cause, we must still understand there to be a reason. In things that persist, the reason is the nature or essence itself, and in a series of changeable things (if, a-priori, we imagine it to be eternal), the reason would be the superior strength of certain inclinations, as we shall soon see, where the reasons don't necessitate (with absolute or metaphysical necessity, where the contrary implies a contradiction[51]) but incline. From this it follows that even if we assume the eternity of the world, we cannot escape the ultimate and extramundane reason for things, God.

Therefore, the reasons for the world lie hidden in something extra-mundane, different from the chain of states, or from the series of things, the collection of which constitutes the world. And so we must pass from physical or hypothetical necessity, which determines the later things in the world from the earlier, to something which is of absolute or metaphysical necessity, something for which a reason cannot be given. For the present world is physically or hypothetically necessary, but not absolutely or metaphysically necessary. That is, given that it was once such and such, it follows that such and such things will arise in the future. Therefore, since the ultimate ground must be in something which is of metaphysical necessity, and since the reason for an existing thing must come from something that actually exists, it follows that there must exist some one entity of metaphysical necessity, that is, there must be an entity whose essence is existence, and therefore something must exist which differs from the plurality of things, which differs from the world, which we have granted and shown is not of metaphysical necessity.

---

51. Reading 'contraria implicet contradictionem' for 'contraria implicet'.

Furthermore, in order to explain a bit more distinctly how temporal, contingent, or physical truths arise from eternal, essential or metaphysical truths, we must first acknowledge that since something rather than nothing exists, there is a certain urge for existence or (so to speak) a straining toward existence in possible things or in possibility or essence itself; in a word, essence in and of itself strives for existence. Futhermore, it follows from this that all possibles, that is, everything that expresses essence or possible reality, strive with equal right for existence[52] in proportion to the amount of essence or reality or the degree of perfection they contain, for perfection is nothing but the amount of essence.

From this it is obvious that of the infinite combinations of possibilities and possible series, the one that exists is the one through which the most essence or possibility is brought into existence. In practical affairs one always follows the decision rule in accordance with which one ought to seek the maximum or the minimum: namely, one prefers the maximum effect at the minimum cost, so to speak. And in this context, time, place, or in a word, the receptivity or capacity of the world can be taken for the cost or the plot of ground on which the most pleasing building possible is to be built, and the variety of shapes [therein] [*formarum . . . varietates*] corresponds to the pleasingness of the building and the number and elegance of the rooms. And the situation is like that in certain games, in which all places on the board are supposed to be filled in accordance with certain rules, where at the end, blocked by certain spaces, you will be forced to leave more places empty than you could have or wanted to, unless you used some trick. There is, however, a certain procedure through which one can most easily fill the board. Thus, if, for example, we suppose that we are directed to construct a triangle, without being given any other directions, the result is that an equilateral triangle would be drawn; and if we suppose that we are to go from one point to another, without being directed to use a particular path, the path chosen will be the easiest or the shortest one. And so, assuming that at some time being is to prevail over nonbeing, or that there is a reason why something rather than nothing is to exist, or that something is to pass from possibility to actuality, although nothing beyond this is determined, it follows that there would be as much as there possibly can be, given the capacity of time and space (that is, the capacity of the order of possible existence); in a word, it is just like tiles laid down so as to contain as many as possible in a given area.

---

52. Reading '*existentiam*' for '*essentiam*'.

From this we can already understand in a wondrous way how a certain Divine Mathematics or Metaphysical Mechanism is used in the very origination of things, and how the determination of a maximum finds a place. The case is like that in geometry, where the straight angle is distinguished from all angles, or like the case of a liquid placed in another of a different kind, which forms itself into the most capacious shape, namely that of a sphere, or best of all, like the case in common mechanics where the struggling of many heavy bodies with one another finally gives rise to a motion through which there results the greatest descent, taken as a whole. For just as all possibles strive with equal right for existence in proportion to their reality, so too all heavy things strive with equal right to descend in proportion to their heaviness, and just as the one case results in the motion which contains as much descent of heavy things as is possible, the other case gives rise to a world in which the greatest number of possibles is produced.

And so, we now have physical necessity derived from metaphysics.[53] For even if the world is not metaphysically necessary, in the sense that its contrary implies a contradiction or a logical absurdity, it is, however, physically necessary or determined, in the sense that its contrary implies imperfection or moral absurdity. And just as possibility is the foundation [*principium*] of essence, so perfection or degree of essence (through which the greatest number of things are compossible) is the foundation of existence. From this it is at the same time obvious how the Author of the World can be free, even though everything happens determinately, since he acts from a principle of wisdom or perfection. Indeed, indifference arises from ignorance, and the wiser one is, the more one is determined to do that which is most perfect.

But, you say, this comparison between a certain determining metaphysical mechanism and the physical mechanism of heavy bodies, though it seems elegant, is faulty insofar as the heavy bodies striving really exist, while possibilities or essences before, or rather outside of existence, are imaginary or fictional, and therefore, one cannot seek a reason for existence in them. I respond that neither those essences nor the so-called eternal truths pertaining to them are fictitious. Rather, they exist in a certain realm of ideas, so to speak, namely, in God himself, the source of every essence and of the existence of the rest. The very existence of the actual series of things

---

53. Leibniz's Latin is ambiguous here; he can also be read as claiming that physical necessity is drawn from metaphysical necessity.

shows that we seem not to have spoken without grounds. For the reason for things must be sought in metaphysical necessities or in eternal truths, since (as I showed above) it cannot be found in the actual series of things. But existing things cannot derive from anything but existing things, as I already noted above. So it is necessary that eternal truths have their existence in a certain absolute or metaphysically necessary subject, that is, in God, through whom those things which would otherwise be imaginary are realized, to use a barbaric but graphic expression.[54]

And indeed, we observe that everything in the world takes place in accordance with laws that are eternally true, laws that are not merely geometrical, but also metaphysical, that is, not only in accordance with material necessities, but also in accordance with formal reasons. This is true not only in very general terms, in the explanation [ratio] we have just now given for why the world exists rather than not, and why it exists this way rather than some other way (which is certainly to be sought in the striving of possibles for existence), but in descending to particulars we also see the wonderful way in which metaphysical laws of cause, power and action, have their place in the whole of nature, and we see that these metaphysical laws prevail over the purely geometrical laws of matter. As I found to my great astonishment in explaining the laws of motion, this is true to such an extent that I was finally forced to abandon the law of the geometrical composition of conatus, which I once defended in my youth, when I was more materialistic, as I have explained at greater length elsewhere.[55]

And so, the ultimate reason for the reality of both essences and existences lies in one thing, which must of necessity be greater than the world, higher than the world, and must have existed before the world did, since through it not only existing things, which make up the world, but also possibles have their reality. Moreover, it can be sought in but one source, because of the interconnection among all of these things. Furthermore, it is obvious that, from this source, things are continually flowing forth, are being produced and were produced, since it is not clear why one state of the world any more than another, yesterday's any more than today's, should flow from it. It is also obvious how God acts not only physically, but freely, how in him there is not only the efficient cause of things, but the final cause, and how in him we have not only the reason for the

---

54. 'Realiso,' the verb Leibniz uses for 'realize' or 'make real,' is corrupt Latin.
55. See A Specimen of Dynamics, AG 117–38.

greatness or power in the mechanism of the universe as now constituted, but also the reason for the goodness or wisdom in constituting
it.

And lest anyone think that I am here confusing moral perfection
or goodness with metaphysical perfection or greatness, and grant the
latter while denying the former, one must realize that it follows from
what I have said that not only is the world physically (or, if you
prefer, metaphysically) most perfect, that is, that the series of things
which has been brought forth is the one in which there is, in actuality,
the greatest amount of reality, but it also follows that the world is
morally most perfect, since moral perfection is in reality physical
perfection with respect to minds. From this it follows that the world
is not only the most admirable machine, but insofar as it is made up
of minds, it is also the best republic, the republic through which
minds derive the greatest possible happiness and joy, in which their
physical perfection consists.

But, you ask, don't we experience quite the opposite in the world?
For the worst often happens to the best, and not only innocent beasts
but also humans are injured and killed, even tortured. In the end,
the world appears to be a certain confused chaos rather than a thing
ordered by some supreme wisdom, especially if one takes note of the
conduct of the human race. I confess that it appears this way at first
glance, but a deeper look at things forces us to quite the contrary
view. From those very considerations which I brought forward it is
obvious *a priori* that everything, even minds, is of the highest perfection there can be.

And indeed, it is unjust to make a judgment unless one has exam-
ined the entire law, as lawyers say. We know but a small part of the
eternity which extends without measure, for how short is the memory
of several thousand years which history gives us. But yet, from such
meager experience we rashly make judgments about the immense
and the eternal, like people born and raised in prison or, if you prefer,
in the subterranean saltmines of the Sarmatians, people who think
that there is no light in the world but the dim light of their torches,
light scarcely sufficient to guide their steps. Look at a very beautiful
picture, and cover it up except for some small part. What will it
look like but some confused combination of colors, without delight,
without art; indeed the more closely we examine it the more it will
look that way. But as soon as the covering is removed, and you see
the whole surface from an appropriate place, you will understand
that what looked like accidental splotches on the canvas were made
with consummate skill by the creator of the work. What the eyes

discover in the painting, the ears discover in music. Indeed, the most distinguished masters of composition quite often mix dissonances with consonances in order to arouse the listener, and pierce him, as it were, so that, anxious about what is to happen, the listener might feel all the more pleasure when order is soon restored, just as we delight in small dangers or in the experience of misfortune for the very feeling or manifestation they provide of our power or happiness, or just as we delight in the spectacle of ropewalkers or sword dancing for their very ability to incite fear, or just as we ourselves laughingly half toss children, as if we are about to throw them off. (It was also for this reason that when Christian, King of Denmark, was still an infant, wrapped in swaddling clothes, an ape carried him to the edge of the roof, and then, while all were in distress, the ape, almost as if he were laughing, put him safely back into the cradle.) On that same principle it is insipid to always eat sweet things; sharp, acidic, and even bitter tastes should be mixed in to stimulate the palate. He who hasn't tasted bitter things hasn't earned sweet things, nor, indeed, will he appreciate them. Pleasure does not derive from uniformity, for uniformity brings forth disgust and makes us dull, not happy: this very principle is a law of delight.

But what we said about the part, which can be disordered without detracting from the harmony of the whole, should not be taken to mean that there is no reason for the parts, or that it would be (as it were) sufficient for the world as a whole to be perfect of its kind, even if the human race were miserable, and no attention paid to justice in the universe, or no provision made for us, as certain persons of poor judgment believe about the totality of things.[56] For one must realize that just as in the best constituted republic, care is taken that each individual gets what is good for him, as much as possible, similarly, the universe would be insufficiently perfect unless it took individuals into account as much as could be done consistently with preserving the harmony of the universe. It is impossible in this matter to find a better standard than the very law of justice, which dictates that everyone should take part in the perfection of the universe and in his own happiness in proportion to his own virtue and to the extent that his will has thus contributed to the common good. This exonerates what we call the charity and love of God, in which the entire force and power of the Christian religion alone consists, in the judgment of wise theologians. Nor should the fact that minds get such deference in the universe appear astonishing, since they are

---

56. See, e.g., Spinoza, appendix to *Ethics* I.

produced in the exact image of the Supreme Creator, and relate to him not only as machines to their builder (as other things do), but also as citizens to their prince. Likewise, they are to persist as long as the universe itself does, and they express the whole in a certain way and concentrate it in themselves, so that it might be said that they are parts that are wholes.

We must also hold that afflictions, especially those the good have, only lead to their greater good. This is true not only in theology, but in nature [*physice*] as well, since a seed flung to the ground must suffer before it bears fruit. And, all in all, one can say that afflictions that are bad in the short run are good in their effect, since they constitute a short path to greater perfection. It is just as in physics, where liquids that ferment slowly also improve more slowly, but those in which there is more violent disturbance improve more quickly because they eliminate [impure] parts with greater force. And this is what you might call stepping back in order to leap forward with greater force (one retreats the better to leap forward). These considerations must be held to be not only pleasing and consoling, but most true. I think that in the universe nothing is truer than happiness, nor is anything happier or sweeter than truth.

In addition to the beauties and perfections of the totality of the divine works, we must also recognize a certain constant and unbounded progress in the whole universe, so that it always proceeds to greater development [*cultus*], just as a large portion of our world is now cultivated [*cultura*] and will become more and more so. And while certain things regress to their original wild state and others are destroyed and buried, we must, however, understand this in the same way that we interpreted affliction a bit earlier. Indeed, this very destruction and burying leads us to the attainment of something better, so that we make a profit from the very loss, in a sense.

And there is a ready answer to the objection that if this were so, then the world should have become Paradise long ago. Many substances have already attained great perfection. However, because of the infinite divisibility of the continuum, there are always parts asleep in the abyss of things, yet to be roused and yet to be advanced to greater and better things, advanced, in a word, to greater cultivation. Thus, progress never comes to an end.

Preface to the New Essays (1703–05)[57]

Leibniz became acquainted with the outline of John Locke's Essay Concerning Human Understanding *before it was actually published, through an abstract of the book, written by Locke, translated into French, and published in Le Clerc's* Bibliothèque Universelle *(1688). When the* Essay *was published in 1690, Leibniz read it in English and sent some criticisms of it to Locke through Thomas Burnet (ca. 1635–1715) and Lady Masham (1658–1708). When, in 1700, Pierre Coste's French translation of the* Essay *was published, Leibniz was able to make a thorough study of it; he planned to publish his critique under the title* New Essays on the Understanding. *When Locke died in 1704, Leibniz abandoned his project to publish the work.*

SINCE THE *Essays on the Understanding*, published by an illustrious Englishman, is one of the finest and most esteemed works of our age, I resolved to comment on it, insofar as I had given sufficient thought for some time to the same subject and to most of the matters touched upon there; I thought that this would be a good opportunity to publish something entitled *New Essays on the Understanding* and to procure a more favorable reception for my thoughts by putting them in such good company. I further thought that I might profit from someone else's work, not only to make my task easier (since, in fact, it is easier to follow the thread of a good author than to work out everything anew), but also to add something to what he has given us, which is always easier than starting from the beginning. It is true that I often hold an opinion different from his, but far from denying on that account the merit of this famous writer, I bear witness to it by showing in what and why, I differ from his view, when I deem it necessary to prevent his authority from prevailing against reason on some important points.

In fact, although the author of the *Essay* says a thousand fine things of which I approve, our systems are very different. His bears more relation to Aristotle's and mine to Plato's, although we both differ in many ways from the doctrines of these two ancients. He is more popular while I am forced at times to be a little more esoteric and abstract, which is not an advantage to me, especially when writing in a living language. However, I believe that by making two characters

---

57. A VI, 6, 43–68; G V 41–61. French.

speak, one of whom presents the views of the author of the *Essay*, while the other adds my observations, the parallel will be more to the liking of the reader than some dry remarks, whose reading would have to be interrupted at every moment by the necessity of having to return to the author's book in order to understand mine. Nevertheless, it would be good to compare our writings from time to time, and to judge his views by his work alone, even though I have usually retained his expressions. It is true that the constraint of having to follow the thread of someone else's discourse in making my remarks has meant that I could not think of capturing the charm of which the dialogue is capable, but I hope that the content will make up for the defect in style.

Our differences are about subjects of some importance. There is the question about whether the soul in itself is completely empty like tablets upon which nothing has been written (*tabula rasa*), as Aristotle and the author of the *Essay* maintain, and whether everything inscribed on it comes solely from the senses and from experience, or whether the soul contains from the beginning the source [*principe*] of several notions and doctrines, which external objects awaken only on certain occasions, as I believe with Plato and even with the Schoolmen, and with all those who find this meaning in the passage of St. Paul (Romans 2:15) where he states that the law of God is written in our hearts. The Stoics call these principles *Prolepses*, that is, fundamental assumptions, or what is taken as agreed in advance. Mathematicians call them *common notions*, (*koinai ennoiai*). Modern philosophers give them other fine names, and Julius Scaliger in particular called them the seeds of eternity, and also *zopyra*, meaning living fires, or flashes of light hidden inside us but made to appear through the contact of the senses, like sparks that can be struck from a steel. And it is not unreasonable to believe that these flashes reveal something divine and eternal, something that especially appears in necessary truths. This raises another question, namely, whether all truths depend upon experience, that is, upon induction and instances, or whether some of them also have another foundation. For if some occurrences can be foreseen before they have been tested, it is obvious that we contribute something of our own here. Although the senses are necessary for all our actual knowledge, they are not sufficient to give us all of it, since the senses never give us anything but instances, that is, particular or individual truths. Now all the instances confirming a general truth, however numerous they may be, are not sufficient to establish the universal necessity of that same truth, for it does no⸀ follow that what has happened before will always happen in the sam way. For example, the Greeks, Romans, and all other people of the earth have always observed that before the passage of twenty-four hours, day changes into night and night into day. But they would have been mistaken if they had believed that the same rule is observed everywhere, since the contrary was observed during a visit to Nova Zembla. And anyone who believed that this is a necessary and eternal truth, at least in our climate, would also be mistaken, since we must recognize that the earth and even the sun do not exist necessarily, and that there may be a time when this beautiful star will no longer exist, at least in its present form, and neither will its whole system. As a result it appears that necessary truths, such as we find in pure mathematics and particularly in arithmetic and geometry, must have principles whose proof does not depend on instances nor, consequently, on the testimony of the senses, although without the senses it would never occur to us to think of them. This is a distinction that should be noted carefully, and it is one Euclid understood so well that he proves by reason things that are sufficiently evident through experience and sensible images. Logic, together with metaphysics and morals, of which the one shapes natural theology and the other natural jurisprudence, are full of such truths, and consequently, their proof can only arise from internal principles, which are called innate. It is true that we must not imagine that we can read these eternal laws of reason in the soul from an open book, as the edict of the praetor can be read from his tablet without effort and scrutiny. But it is enough that they can be discovered in us by dint of attention; the senses furnish occasions for this, and the success of experiments also serves to confirm reason, a bit like empirical trials help us avoid errors of calculation in arithmetic when the reasoning is long. Also, it is in this respect that human knowledge differs from that of beasts. Beasts are purely empirical and are guided solely by instances, for, as far as we are able to judge, they never manage to form necessary propositions, whereas man is capable of demonstrative knowledge [*sciences demonstratives*]. In this, the faculty beasts have for drawing consequences is inferior to the reason humans have. The consequences beasts draw are just like those of simple empirics, who claim that what has happened will happen again in a case where what strikes them is similar, without being able to determine whether the same reasons are at work. This is what makes it so easy for men to capture beasts, and so easy for simple empirics to make mistakes. Not even people made skillful by age and experience are exempt from this when they rely too much on their past experiences. This has happened to several people in civil and military affairs, since they do not take sufficiently into consideration the fact that the world changes and that men have become more skillful in finding thousands of new tricks, unlike the stags and hares of today, who have not become any more clever than those of yesterday. The consequences beasts draw are only a shadow of reasoning, that is, they are only connections of imagination, transitions from one image to another; for, when a new situation appears similar to the preceding one, they expect to find again what was previously joined to it, as though things were linked in fact, just because their images are linked in the memory. It is, indeed, true that reason ordinarily counsels us to expect that we will find in the future that which conforms to our long experience of the past; but this is not, on that account, a necessary and infallible truth, and it can fail us when we least expect it, when the reasons which have maintained it change. This is why the wisest people do not rely on it to such an extent that they do not try to probe into the reason for what happens (if that is possible), so as to judge when exceptions must be made. For only reason is capable of establishing sure rules and of providing what uncertain rules lack by formulating exceptions to them, and lastly, capable of finding connections that are certain in the compulsiveness [*force*] of necessary consequences. This often provides a way of foreseeing an occurrence without having to experience the sensible links between images, which the beasts are reduced to doing. Thus what justifies the internal principles of necessary truths also distinguishes humans from beasts.

Perhaps our able author will not entirely disagree with my opinion. For after having devoted his whole first book to rejecting innate illumination, understood in a certain way, he admits, however, at the beginning of the second book and in what follows, that the ideas which do not originate in sensation come from reflection. Now, reflection is nothing other than attention to what is within us, and the senses do not give us what we already bring with us. Given this, can anyone deny that there is a great deal innate in our mind, since we are innate to ourselves, so to speak, and since we have within ourselves being, unity, substance, duration, change, action, perception, pleasure, and a thousand other objects of our intellectual ideas? And since these objects are immediate and always present to our understanding (though they may not always be perceived consciously [*apperçus*] on account of our distractions and our needs), why should it be surprising that we say that these ideas, and everything that depends upon them, are innate in us? I have also used the comparison with a block of veined marble, rather than a completely uniform block of marble, or an empty tablet, that is, what the philosophers call a *tabula rasa*. For if the soul were like these empty tablets, truths would be in us as the shape of Hercules is in a block of marble, when the marble is completely indifferent to receiving this shape or another. But if the stone had veins which marked out the shape of Hercules rather than other shapes, then that block would be more determined with respect to that shape and Hercules would be as though innate in it in some sense, even though some labor would be required for these veins to be exposed and polished into clarity by the removal of everything that prevents them from appearing. This is how ideas and truths are innate in us, as natural inclinations, dispositions, habits, or potentialities [*virtualités*] are, and not as actions are, although these potentialities are always accompanied by some corresponding, though often insensible, actions.

Our able author seems to claim that there is nothing *potential* [*virtuel*] in us, and even nothing that we are not always actually conscious of perceiving [*appercevions*]. But he cannot hold this in all strictness; otherwise his position would be too paradoxical, since, again, acquired habits and the contents of our memory are not always consciously perceived [*apperçues*] and do not even always come to our aid when needed, though often we easily recall them to mind when some trivial occasion reminds us of them, as when we need only the beginning of a song to make us remember the rest. He also limits his thesis in other places, saying that there is nothing in us that we did not at least previously perceive consciously [*apperçu*]. But no one can guarantee by reason alone how far back our past and perhaps forgotten apperceptions can go, especially in view of the Platonists' doctrine of reminiscence, which, fabulous though it is, is not at all incompatible with pure reason. Furthermore, why must it be that everything is acquired by apperceptions of external things and that nothing can be unearthed from within ourselves? Is our soul in itself so empty that, without images borrowed from the outside, it is nothing? This is not, I am convinced, a view our judicious author could approve. Where could one find some tablets which do not have a certain amount of variety in themselves? Will we ever see a perfectly homogeneous and uniform surface? Then why could we not also provide ourselves some object of thought from our own depths, when we are willing to dig there? Thus I am led to believe that, fundamentally, his view on this point is no different from mine, or rather from the common view, insofar as he recognizes two sources of our knowledge, the senses and reflection.

I do not know whether it will be as easy to reconcile him with me and with the Cartesians when he maintains that the mind does not

always think, and in particular, that it is without perception during
dreamless sleep, and when he objects that since bodies can be without
motion, souls can just as well be without thought. But here I reply
somewhat differently from what is customary. For I maintain that a
substance cannot naturally be without action, and that there is never
even any body without motion. Experience already supports me, and
to be convinced of this, one need only consult the book of the
illustrious Mr. Boyle against absolute rest.[58] But I believe that reason
also supports this, and it is one of the proofs I use for refuting atoms.
Moreover, there are a thousand indications that allow us to judge
that at every moment there is an infinity of perceptions in us, but
without apperception and without reflection—that is, changes in
the soul itself, which we do not consciously perceive [appercevons],
because these impressions are either too small or too numerous, or
too homogeneous, in the sense that they have nothing sufficiently
distinct in themselves; but combined with others, they do have their
effect and make themselves felt in the assemblage, at least confusedly.
It is in this way that custom makes us ignore the motion of a mill or
of a waterfall, after we have lived nearby for some time. It is not that
this motion ceases to strike our organs and that there is nothing
corresponding to it in the soul, on account of the harmony of the soul
and the body, but that the impressions in the soul and in the body,
lacking the appeal of novelty, are not sufficiently strong to attract our
attention and memory, which are applied only to more demanding
objects. All attention requires memory, and when we are not alerted,
so to speak, to pay heed to some of our own present perceptions, we
let them pass without reflection and without even noticing them. But
if someone alerts us to them right away and makes us take note, for
example, of some noise we have just heard, we remember it, and we
consciously perceive that we just had some sensation of it. Thus there
were perceptions that we did not consciously perceive right away,
the apperception in this case arising only after an interval, however
brief. In order better to recognize [juger] these tiny perceptions [petites
perceptions] that cannot be distinguished in a crowd, I usually make
use of the example of the roar or noise of the sea that strikes us when
we are at the shore. In order to hear this noise as we do, we must
hear the parts that make up this whole, that is, we must hear the
noise of each wave, even though each of these small noises is known
only in the confused assemblage of all the others, and would not be
noticed if the wave making it were the only one. For we must be

---

58. Robert Boyle, *Discourse about the Absolute Rest in Bodies* (1669).

slightly affected by the motion of this wave, and we must have some perception of each of these noises, however small they may be, otherwise we would not have the noise of a hundred thousand waves, since a hundred thousand nothings cannot make something. Moreover, we never sleep so soundly that we do not have some weak and confused sensation, and we would never be awakened by the greatest noise in the world if we did not have some perception of its beginning, small as it might be, just as we could never break a rope by the greatest effort in the world, unless it were stretched and strained slightly by the least efforts, even though the slight extension they produce is not apparent.

These tiny perceptions are therefore more effectual than one thinks. They make up this I-know-not-what, those flavors, those images of the sensory qualities, clear in the aggregate but confused in their parts; they make up those impressions the surrounding bodies make on us, which involve the infinite, and this connection that each being has with the rest of the universe. It can even be said that as a result of these tiny perceptions, the present is filled with the future and laden with the past, that everything conspires together (*sympnoia panta*, as Hippocrates said), and that eyes as piercing as those of God could read the whole sequence of the universe in the smallest of substances.

The things that are, the things that have been, and the things that will soon be brought in by the future.[59]

These insensible perceptions also indicate and constitute the individual, which is individuated [*caractérise*] by the traces which these perceptions preserve of its previous states, connecting it up with his present state. They can be known by a superior mind, even when the individual himself does not sense them, that is, when he no longer has an explicit memory of them. But these perceptions even provide a way of recovering the memory, as needed, through periodic unfoldings which may occur one day. That is why death might only be a state of sleep, and might not even remain one, insofar as the perceptions merely cease to be sufficiently distinct and, in animals, are reduced to a state of confusion which suspends apperception, but which cannot last forever; I shall not speak here of man, who ought to have great prerogatives in this matter in order to retain his personality.

It is also by means of these insensible perceptions that I explain the marvelous pre-established harmony between the soul and the

---

59. Virgil, *Georgics* IV 393.

body, and also between all the monads or simple substances, which takes the place of that untenable influence of the one on the others, and which, in the judgment of the author of the finest of dictionaries,[60] raises the greatness of divine perfections beyond anything ever conceived before. After this I would add little if I said that it is these tiny perceptions which determine us in many situations without our thinking of them, and which deceive the common people by giving the appearance of an *indifference of equilibrium*, as if it made no difference to us, for example, whether we turned right or left. Nor is it necessary for me to point out here, as I've done in the book itself,[61] that they cause this uneasiness, which I show to consist in something that differs from pain only as the small differs from the great, and yet which often brings about our desire and even our pleasure by giving it a kind of spice. The insensible parts of our sensible perceptions also bring about a relation between those perceptions of color, heat, and other sensible qualities, and the motions in bodies that correspond to them. But the Cartesians and our author, penetrating though he is, think of the perceptions we have of these qualities as arbitrary, that is, as if God had given them to the soul according to his good pleasure without having regard to any essential relation between perceptions and their objects, a view which surprises me and seems to me unworthy of the wisdom of the author of things, who does nothing without harmony and reason.

In short, *insensible perceptions* have as much use in philosophy of mind [*Pneumatique*] as corpuscles do in physics; and it is equally unreasonable to reject the one as the other under the pretext that they are beyond the reach of the senses. Nothing takes place all at once, and it is one of the greatest and best verified maxims that *nature never makes leaps*; this is what I called *the law of continuity* when I once spoke about this in the *Nouvelles de la république des lettres*,[62] and this law is of considerable use in physics. It entails that one always passes from the small to the large and back again through what lies between, both in degrees and in parts, and that a motion never arises immediately from rest nor is it reduced to rest except through a lesser motion, just as we never manage to pass through any

---

60. Pierre Bayle. The reference is to Bayle's discussion of Leibniz in notes H and L to the article "Rorarius" in his *Dictionary*. Bayle's point is that Leibniz's pre-established harmony puts implausibly severe demands on God's power.
61. In the *New Essays* II.23.
62. The reference is to "A Letter of Mr. Leibniz on a General Principle Useful in explaining the Laws of Nature . . . ," which appeared in the July 1687 issue of the *Nouvelles*, and is translated in L 351–53.

line or length before having passed through a shorter one. But until now, those who have given the laws of motion have not observed this law, believing that a body can instantaneously receive a motion opposite to the previous motion. All this can allow us to judge that noticeable perceptions arise by degrees from ones too small to be noticed. To judge otherwise is to know little of the immense subtlety of things, which always and everywhere involves an actual infinity.

I have also noticed that because of insensible variations, two individual things cannot be perfectly alike and must always differ in something over and above number. This puts an end to the empty tablets of the soul, a soul without thought, a substance without action, void space, atoms, and even particles in matter not actually divided, complete uniformity in a part of time, place, or matter, the perfect globes of the second element that derive from the perfect original cubes, and a thousand other fictions of philosophers which arise from their incomplete notions. These are things that the nature of things does not allow, things that are allowed to pass because of our ignorance and lack of attention; they cannot be tolerated unless we limit them to being abstractions of the mind, which protests that it does not deny the things it sets aside, but only judges that they need not enter into consideration at present. If we thought in earnest that things we do not consciously perceive [*s'apperçoit*] are not in the soul or in the body, we would fail in philosophy as in politics, by neglecting the *mikron*, imperceptible changes. But an abstraction is not an error, provided we know that what we are ignoring is really there. This is similar to what mathematicians do when they talk about the perfect lines they propose to us, uniform motions and other regular effects, although *matter* (that is, the mixture of the effects of the surrounding infinity) always provides some exception. We proceed in this way in order to distinguish various considerations and, as far as is possible, to reduce effects to their reasons, and foresee some of their consequences. For the more careful we are not to neglect any consideration we can subject to rules [*reguler*], the more closely practice corresponds to theory. But only the supreme reason, which nothing escapes, can distinctly understand the whole infinite, all the reasons, and all the consequences. With respect to infinities, we can only know them confusedly, but at least we can distinctly know that they exist, otherwise we would be very poor judges of the beauty and greatness of the universe, just as we would also be unable to develop a good physics which explains the nature of things in general, and still less a good philosophy of mind [*Pneumatique*], which includes the knowledge of God, of souls, and of simple substances in general.

This knowledge of insensible perceptions also serves to explain why and how two souls of the same species, whether human or otherwise, never leave the hands of the creator perfectly alike, and why and how each of them always has its original relation to the point of view it will have in the universe. But this already follows from what I pointed out previously about two individuals, namely that the *difference* between them is always *more than numerical*. There is another significant point on which I must differ, not only from the opinion of our author, but also from those of most of the moderns. I hold with most of the ancients that all spiritual beings [*génies*], all souls, all simple created substances, are always joined to a body, and that souls are never completely separated from bodies. I have *a priori* reasons for this, but this doctrine will be found to have the further advantage that it resolves all the philosophical difficulties about the state of souls, their perpetual conservation, their immortality, and their operation. Since the difference between one of their states and another is never, nor has it ever been anything but the difference between the more and the less sensible, between the more and the less perfect (or the other way around), the past or future state of souls is just as explicable as their present one. The slightest reflection is sufficient to show that this is reasonable, and that a leap from one state to an infinitely different one cannot be natural. I am surprised that the schools, by needlessly abandoning nature, have been willing to readily plunge into enormous difficulties, and thus to give free thinkers [*esprits forts*] an opportunity for their apparent triumphs. The arguments of the free thinkers collapse all at once with this explanation of things, in which it is no more difficult to conceive the preservation of souls (or rather, on my view, of the animal), than it is to conceive the change from caterpillar to butterfly and the preservation of thought in sleep, to which Jesus Christ has divinely compared death.[63] Also, I have already said that no sleep can last forever; but it will have less duration or almost no duration at all in the case of rational souls, which are always destined to remain the persons [*personnage*] they were in the city of God, and consequently, to retain their memory, so that they can be better able to receive rewards and punishments. I further add that, in general, no disordering of its visible organs is capable of bringing things in the animal to the point of complete confusion, or to destroy all its organs, and to deprive the soul of the whole of its organic body and of the ineradicable remains of all its preceding traces. But the ease with which people

---

63. John 11:11.

have abandoned the ancient doctrine that angels have subtle bodies (a doctrine which has been confused with the corporality of angels), the introduction of the allegedly separated intelligences among created things (to which the intelligences that rotated Aristotle's heavens have contributed much), and finally the poorly understood opinion some have held that we cannot retain the souls of beasts without falling into metempsychosis, all these in my opinion have resulted in the neglect of the natural way of explaining the preservation of the soul. This has done great harm to natural religion, and has led many to believe that our immortality is nothing but a miraculous grace of God. Our celebrated author speaks with some doubt about this, as I will soon point out. But I wish that all who are of this opinion discussed it as wisely and as sincerely as he does. For it is to be feared that several who speak of immortality through grace merely do so in order to preserve appearances, and are at bottom not very far from those Averroists and certain pernicious Quietists who imagine an absorption and reunion of the soul with the ocean of divinity, a notion whose impossibility is clearly shown by my system alone, perhaps.

It seems, moreover, that we also disagree about matter, insofar as the author judges that the void is necessary for motion, since he believes that the small parts of matter are rigid. I admit that if matter were composed of such parts, motion in a plenum would be impossible; it would be as if a room were filled with a quantity of little pebbles without containing the least empty place. But I cannot grant this assumption, for which there seems to be no reasoñ, even though this able author goes so far as to believe that the rigidity or the cohesion of the small parts constitutes the essence of bodies. Rather, we should conceive of space as filled with matter that was originally fluid, matter capable of any division, and indeed, actually subjected to division and subdivision to infinity, but with this difference, however, that it is unequally divisible and unequally divided in different places because of the motions there, motions which are already more or less harmonious. This brings it about that it has rigidity as well as fluidity everywhere, and that no body is hard or fluid to the ultimate degree, that is, that no atom has insuperable hardness, nor is any mass entirely indifferent to division. The order of nature, and particularly the law of continuity, also destroys both alternatives equally well.

I have also shown that *cohesion*, which is not itself an effect of impulsion or motion, would cause *traction*, properly speaking. For if there were an originally rigid body, an Epicurean atom, for example, which had a part projecting in the form of a hook (since we can imagine atoms in all sorts of shapes), this hook when pushed would pull with it the rest of the atom, that is to say, the part not pushed and not falling within the line of the impulse. However, our able author is himself opposed to those philosophic tractions, like the ones formerly attributed to the fear of the void, and he reduces them to impulses, maintaining with the moderns that one part of matter operates on another only by pushing against it from close by. I think that they are right about this, because otherwise the operation would not be intelligible at all.

I must not, however, conceal the fact that I have noticed a kind of retraction on this point on the part of our excellent author, and I cannot refrain from praising his modest sincerity about it, just as I have admired his penetrating insight on other occasions. His retraction occurs on page 408 of the reply to the second letter of the late Bishop of Worcester, printed in 1699. There, in order to justify the view he maintained against this learned prelate, namely that matter is capable of thought, he says among other things: *It is true, I say* *"that bodies operate by impulse and nothing else"* (*Essay*, II, chap. 8, sec. 11). *And so I thought when I writ it, and can yet conceive no other way of their operation. But I am since convinced by the judicious Mr. Newton's incomparable book, that it is too bold a presumption to limit God's power, [in this point], by our narrow conceptions. The gravitation of matter towards matter, by ways inconceivable to me, is not only a demonstration that God can, if he pleases, put into bodies powers and ways of operation, above what can be derived from our idea of body or can be explained by what we know of matter, but also an unquestionable [and everywhere visible] instance, that he has actually done so. And therefore, in the next edition of my book I shall take care to have that passage rectified.*[64] I find in the French version of this book, which was no doubt taken from the latest editions, that sec. 11 reads thus: *It is manifest, at least insofar as we can conceive it, that it is by impulse and nothing else that bodies operate one upon another, it being impossible to conceive that body should operate on what it does not touch, which is all one to imagine that it can operate where it is not.*[65]

I can only praise the modest piety of our famous author, who

---

64. *Works* III, 467–68. The two passages in the brackets were omitted in Leibniz's French translation of Locke's text. In addition, Locke talks of "my narrow conceptions" rather than "our narrow conceptions."

65. Leibniz is referring here to Pierre Coste's translation, *Essai Philosophique Concernant l'Entendement Humain*. Published in 1700, the same year as the important 4th edition of the *Essay*, it represents an intermediate stage between the 3rd and 4th editions. See *Essay*, ed. Nidditch, pp. xxxiv–xxxvi.

recognizes that God can do what goes beyond our understanding, and thus, that there may be inconceivable mysteries in the articles of faith. But I would not want us to be obliged to appeal to miracles in the ordinary course of nature, and to admit absolutely inexplicable powers and operations there. Otherwise, on the strength of what God can do, we would grant too much license to bad philosophers, allowing them those *centripetal virtues* or those *immediate attractions* at a distance, without it being possible to make them intelligible; I do not see what would prevent our Scholastics from saying that everything happens simply through faculties and from maintaining their intentional species, which go from objects to us and find a way of entering our souls. If this is acceptable,

What I said could not be will now happen.[66]

So it seems to me that our author, judicious as he is, is here going rather too much from one extreme to the other. He raises difficulties about the operations of *souls*, when it is merely a matter of admitting what is not *sensible*, while here he grants *bodies* what is not even *intelligible*, allowing them powers and actions beyond everything which, in my opinion, a created mind could do or understand; for he grants them attraction, even at great distances, without limitation to any sphere of activity, and he does so in order to maintain a view which is no less inexplicable, namely the possibility of matter thinking in the natural order of things.[67]

The question he is discussing with the noted prelate who had attacked him is whether *matter can think*. Since this is an important point, and an important point for the present work as well, I cannot avoid going into it a bit, and taking account of their debate. I shall represent the substance of their dispute and take the liberty of saying what I think of it. The late Bishop of Worcester, fearing (but without great cause, in my opinion) that the author's doctrine of ideas was subject to some abuses prejudicial to the Christian faith, undertook to examine some aspects of it in his *Vindication of the Doctrine of the Trinity*. He first gives this excellent writer his due, by recognizing that the writer judges that the existence of the mind is as certain as that of the body, even though as regards these substances, the one is

66. Ovid, *Tristia*, I.7.7.
67. In his notes for the preface, Leibniz wrote: "The philosophy of the author destroys what appears to me to be the most important thing, that the soul is imperishable, whereas on his view there must be a miracle for it to endure. This is directly opposed to the Platonic philosophy joined to that of Democritus and Aristotle, such as mine is." (A VI, 6, 48)

as little known as the other. He then asks (pages 241 seqq.) how
reflection could assure us of the existence of the mind if God can give
matter the faculty of thinking, as our author believes (Book IV, chap.
3, [sec. 6]) since, as a consequence, the way of ideas, which should
serve to discriminate what can belong to the soul or to the body,
would become useless. However, it was said in Book II of the *Essay
on the Understanding* (chap. 23, sec. 15, 27, 28), that the operations
of the soul provide us with the idea of the mind, and that the understanding, together with the will, makes this idea as intelligible to us
as the nature of body is made intelligible by solidity and impulse.
Here is how our author replies to this in his *First Letter* (pp. 65 seqq.):
[[*I think that I have proved that there is a spiritual substance in us.* For]]
*we experiment in ourselves thinking. The idea of this action, or mode of
thinking, is inconsistent with the idea of self-subsistence, and therefore has
a necessary connection with a support or subject of inhesion: the idea of
that support is what we call substance. . . . The general idea of substance
being the same everywhere, the modification of thinking, or the power of
thinking, joined to it, makes it a spirit, without considering what other
modification it has, as whether it has the modification of solidity or not.
As, on the other side, substance, that has the modification of solidity, is
matter, whether it has the modification of thinking or no. And therefore,
if your lordship means by a spiritual, an immaterial substance, I grant I
have not proved, nor upon my principles, can it be proved* [. . .] *that
there is an immaterial substance in us* [. . . .] *Though I presume, what
I have said about the supposition of a system of matter* [. . .] (Book IV,
chap 10, sec. 16) *(which there demonstrates that God is immaterial) will
prove it in the highest degree probable, that the thinking substance in us
is immaterial. . . .*[[*Yet I have shown* (adds the author, p. 68)]] *that all
the great ends of religion and morality are secured . . . by the immortality of
the soul, without a necessary supposition that the soul is immaterial.*[68]

In his *Reply* to this letter, to show that our author was of another
opinion when he wrote Book II of the *Essay*, the learned Bishop
quotes (p. 51) the following passage (Book II, chap. 23, sec. 15),
where it is said that *by the simple ideas we have taken from those
operations of our own minds* [. . .] *we are able to frame the complex
idea of spirit. And thus, by putting together the ideas of thinking, perceiving, liberty, and power of moving our bodies, we have as clear a* [. . .]
notion of immaterial substances as we have of material.[69] He further cites

---

68. *Works* III 33–34. Passages in double brackets are transitional phrases added by
Leibniz.
69. In Locke, it was "themselves" rather than "our bodies." In later editions Leibniz
added "immaterial" to spirit.

other passages to show that the author opposed mind to body. He says (p. 54) that the end of religion and morality is better secured by proving that the soul is immortal by its very nature, that is, immaterial. He further cites this passage (p. 70), that *all the ideas we have of particular, distinct sorts of substances are nothing but several combinations of simple ideas,*[70] and that, consequently, the author believed that the idea of thinking and willing results in a substance different from that given by the idea of solidity and impulse. And he says that in sec. 17 the author remarks that the latter ideas constitute the body as opposed to the mind.

The Bishop of Worcester could have added that from the fact that the *general idea* of substance is in body and in mind, it does not follow that their differences are *modifications* of a single thing, as our author just said in the passage I cited from his *First Letter*. We must distinguish between modifications and attributes. The faculties of having perception and of acting, as well as extension, and solidity, are attributes, or perpetual and principal predicates; but thought, impetuosity, shapes, and motions are modifications of these attributes. Moreover, we must distinguish between the physical (or real) genus and logical (or ideal) genus. The things of the same physical genus, or those which are *homogeneous*, are of the same matter, so to speak, and can often be changed from one into another by changing their modifications, like circles and squares. But two heterogeneous things can have a common logical genus, and then their *differences* are neither simple accidental modifications of a single subject, nor of a single metaphysical or physical matter. Thus time and space are quite heterogeneous things, and we would be wrong to imagine some common real subject I-know-not-what which had only continuous quality in general and whose modifications resulted in time or space. Yet their common logical genus is continuous quantity. Someone might perhaps make fun of these philosophical distinctions between two genera, the one only logical and the other real, and between two matters, the one physical—that of bodies—and the other only metaphysical or general, as if someone were to say that two parts of space are of the same matter or that two hours are also of the same matter as one another. Yet these distinctions concern not only terms, but also things themselves, and seem to be particularly relevant here, where their confusion has given rise to a false conclusion. These two genera have a common notion, and the notion of real genus is common to both sets of matters, so that their genealogy would be as follows:

---

70. *Essay*, II.23.6.

GENUS
$$\begin{cases} \text{the merely } \textit{logical,} \\ \text{distinguished by} \\ \text{simple } \textit{differences} \\ \\ \text{the } \textit{real}, \text{ that is, MATTER,} \\ \text{where differences} \\ \text{are } \textit{modifications} \end{cases}$$

the merely *metaphysical,*
in which
there is homogeneity

the *physical,*
in which there is a
solid, homogeneous mass

I have not seen the author's *Second Letter* to the bishop; the *Reply* that the prelate makes to it hardly touches the point about the thinking of matter. But our author's *Reply* to this *Second Reply* returns to it. *God* (he says, nearly in these words, page 397) *adds the qualities and perfections that please him to the essence of matter; to some parts [he adds] simple motion, to plants vegetation, and to animals sensation. Those who agree with me so far exclaim against me as soon as I go a step further and say that God may give to matter thought, reason, and volition—as if this would destroy the essence of matter. But to prove this assertion they advance that thought or reason is not included in the essence of matter; this proves nothing since motion and life are not included in it either. They also advance that we cannot conceive that matter can think; but our conception is not the measure of God's power.*[71] After this he quotes the example of the attraction of matter (p. 99, but especially p. 408), in which he speaks of the gravitation of matter toward matter, attributed to Mr. Newton, in the words I quoted above, admitting that we can never conceive how this happens. This is, in fact, a return to occult qualities or, what is more, to inexplicable qualities. He adds (p. 401) that nothing is more apt to favor the skeptics than denying what we don't understand, and (p. 402) that we do not even conceive how the soul thinks. He holds (p. 403) that since the two substances, material and immaterial, can be conceived in their bare essence without any activity, it is up to God to give the power of thinking to the one or to the other. And he wants to take advantage of his adversary's view, which grants sensation to beasts, but does not grant them any immaterial substance. He claims that freedom, self-consciousness (p. 408), and the power of making abstractions can be given to matter, not as matter, but as enriched by divine power. Finally he reports

---

71. This is a paraphrase of *Works* III 460–61.

(p. 434) the observation of a traveller as eminent and judicious as Mr. de la Loubere that the pagans of the East know of the immortality of the soul without being able to understand its immateriality.

With regard to all this I will note, before coming to the explanation of my opinion, that it is certain that matter is as little capable of producing sensation mechanically as it is of producing reason, as our author agrees. Furthermore, I note, indeed, that I recognize that we are not allowed to deny what we do not understand, though I add that we have the right to deny (at least in the order of nature) what is absolutely unintelligible and inexplicable. I also maintain that substances (material or immaterial) cannot be conceived in their bare essence without activity, and that activity is of the essence of substance in general. And finally, I maintain that the conception of creatures is not the measure of God's power, but that their conceptivity, or ability [*force*] to conceive, is the measure of nature's power; everything in conformity with the natural order can be conceived or understood by some creature.

Those who understand my system will judge that I will not be in complete agreement with either of these two excellent authors, whose dispute, however, is very instructive. But to explain myself distinctly, one must above all take into account that the modifications which can come naturally or without miracle to a single subject must come to it from the limitations or variations of a real genus or of an original nature, constant and absolute. For this is how in philosophy we distinguish the modes of an absolute being from the being itself; for example, we know that magnitude, shape, and motion are obviously limitations and variations of corporeal nature. For it is clear how a limitation of extension produces shapes, and that the change which takes place there is nothing but motion. And every time we find some quality in a subject, we ought to think that, if we understood the nature of this subject and of this quality, we would understand how this quality could result from that nature. Thus in the order of nature (setting miracles aside) God does not arbitrarily give these or those qualities indifferently to substances; he never gives them any but those which are natural to them, that is to say, those that can be derived from their nature as explicable modifications. Thus we can judge that matter does not naturally have the attraction mentioned above, and does not of itself move on a curved path, because it is not possible to conceive how this takes place, that is to say, it is not possible to explain it mechanically, whereas that which is natural should be capable of becoming distinctly conceivable, if we were admitted into the secrets of things. This distinction between what is natural and explicable and what is inexplicable and miraculous removes all the difficulties: if we were to reject it, we would uphold something worse than occult qualities, and in doing so we would renounce philosophy and reason, and throw open refuges for ignorance and idleness through a hollow system, a system which admits not only that there are qualities we do not understand (of which there are only too many) but also that there are some qualities that the greatest mind could not understand, even if God provided him with every possible advantage, that is, qualities that would be either miraculous or without rhyme or reason. And it would indeed be without rhyme or reason that God should ordinarily perform miracles, so that this do-nothing hypothesis would equally destroy philosophy, which searches for reasons, and the divine wisdom, which provides them.

As for the question of thinking, it is certain—and our author recognizes in more than one place—that thinking cannot be an intelligible modification of matter, that is, that a sensing or thinking being is not a mechanical thing like a watch or a windmill, in the sense that we could conceive of magnitudes, shapes and motions whose mechanical conjunction could produce something thinking, and even sensing, in a mass in which there was nothing of the kind, that would likewise cease to be if the mechanism got out of order. Thus it is not natural for matter to sense and to think, and there are only two ways in which it could do so. One of these would be for God to join to it a substance to which thought is natural, and the other would be for God to endow it with thought miraculously. In this, then, I agree entirely with the Cartesians, except that I extend the view to beasts as well, and believe that they have sensation and souls which are, properly speaking, immaterial and as imperishable as the atoms of Democritus or Gassendi. But the Cartesians, who are confused about the souls of beasts, and do not know what to do with them if they are preserved (since it did not occur to them that the animal might be preserved in a reduced form), have been forced to deny them even sensation, contrary to all appearances, and contrary to the judgment of mankind. But if someone said that God, at very least, can add this faculty of thinking to a mechanism properly prepared, I would answer that if this occurred, and if God added this faculty to matter without at the same time endowing it with a substance that was the subject in which this same faculty inhered (as I conceive it), that is, without adding an immaterial soul there, then matter would have to be raised miraculously so as to be capable of receiving a power of which it is not capable naturally, just as some Scholastics claim that God raises fire to the point of giving it the power directly to burn minds separated from matter, which would be a miracle, pure and simple. It is enough that we can maintain that matter thinks only if we attribute to it either an imperishable soul, or else a miracle, and thus, that the immortality of our souls follows from what is natural, since we could then hold that they are destroyed only by miracle, whether by exalting matter or by annihilating the soul. For we know, of course, that the power of God could make our souls mortal, even though they may be immaterial (or immortal by nature alone), since he is capable of annihilating them.

Now the truth of the immateriality of the soul is undoubtedly important. For it is infinitely more useful to religion and morality, especially in our days (when many people have scant respect for revelation by itself or for miracles), to show that souls are naturally immortal, and that it would be a miracle if they were not, than it would be to maintain that our souls must naturally die, and that it is due to a miraculous grace, based solely on God's promise, that they do not die. Moreover, we have known for a long time that those who wished to destroy natural religion, and reduce everything to revelation, as if reason taught us nothing about it, have been held suspect, and not always without reason. But our author is not of their number. He maintains a demonstration of God's existence and he attributes to the immateriality of the soul *a probability of the highest degree*, which may consequently pass for a *moral certainty*, so that I imagine that, having as much sincerity as penetration, he might quite well come to agree with the doctrine I have just expounded, a doctrine fundamental in every reasonable philosophy. For otherwise, I do not see how we can prevent ourselves from falling back into a fanatical philosophy, such as the *Mosaic philosophy* of Fludd, which saves all phenomena by attributing them immediately and miraculously to God, or into a barbaric philosophy, like that of certain philosophers and physicians of former days, who still savored of the barbarism of their own age, and who today are justly despised. They saved the appearances by explicitly fabricating suitable occult qualities or faculties, which were thought to be like little demons or spirits able to do what was required of them without any fuss, just as if pocket watches told time by some faculty of clockness without the need of wheels, or mills crushed grain by a fractive faculty without the need of anything like millstones. As for the difficulty many people have had in conceiving an immaterial substance, it soon ceases (at least in large part) when one no longer requires substances separated from matter; I hold, in fact, that such substances have never existed naturally among created things.

The Principles of Philosophy, or, the Monadology (1714)[72]

The "Monadology" is one of the most popular of Leibniz's writings, and has shaped our view of his philosophy from the eighteenth century to the present. It should be stressed that the "Monadology" was not intended as an introduction to Leibniz's philosophy, but rather as a condensed statement of the main principles of his philosophy and an elucidation of some of the passages of his Theodicy.

1. THE *MONAD*, which we shall discuss here, is nothing but a simple substance that enters into composites—simple, that is, without parts (*Theodicy*, sec. 10).

2. And there must be simple substances, since there are composites; for the composite is nothing more than a collection, or *aggregate*, of simples.

3. But where there are no parts, neither extension, nor shape, nor divisibility is possible. These monads are the true atoms of nature and, in brief, the elements of things.

4. There is also no dissolution to fear, and there is no conceivable way in which a simple substance can perish naturally.

5. For the same reason, there is no conceivable way a simple substance can begin naturally, since it cannot be formed by composition.

6. Thus, one can say that monads can only begin or end all at once, that is, they can only begin by creation and end by annihilation, whereas composites begin or end through their parts.

7. There is also no way of explaining how a monad can be altered or changed internally by some other creature, since one cannot transpose anything in it, nor can one conceive of any internal motion that can be excited, directed, augmented, or diminished within it, as can be done in composites, where there can be change among the parts. The monads have no windows through which something can enter or leave. Accidents cannot be detached, nor can they go about outside of substances, as the sensible species of the Scholastics once did. Thus, neither substance nor accident can enter a monad from without.[73]

---

72. "Principles . . ." was probably Leibniz's title. RPM and G VI 607–23. French. References to the *Theodicy* are not found in the final copy, but are taken from an earlier draft.

73. Deleted from the first draft: "Monads are not mathematical points. For these points are only extremities, and the line cannot be composed of points."

8. However, monads must have some qualities, otherwise they would not even be beings.[74] And if simple substances did not differ at all in their qualities, there would be no way of perceiving any change in things, since what there is in a composite can only come from its simple ingredients; and if the monads had no qualities, they would be indiscernible from one another, since they also do not differ in quantity. As a result, assuming a plenum, in motion, each place would always receive only the equivalent of what it already had, and one state of things would be indistinguishable from another[75] (Pref.***.2.b).

9. It is also necessary that each monad be different from each other. For there are never two beings in nature that are perfectly alike, two beings in which it is not possible to discover an internal difference, that is, one founded on an intrinsic denomination.

10. I also take for granted that every created being, and consequently the created monad as well, is subject to change, and even that this change is continual in each thing.

11. It follows from what we have just said that the monad's natural changes come from an *internal principle,* since no external cause can influence it internally (sec. 396, 400).

12. But, besides the principle of change, there must be *diversity* [*un détail*] *in that which changes,* which produces, so to speak, the specification and variety of simple substances.

13. This diversity must involve a multitude in the unity or in the simple. For, since all natural change is produced by degrees, something changes and something remains. As a result, there must be a plurality of properties [*affections*] and relations in the simple substance, although it has no parts.

14. The passing state which involves and represents a multitude in the unity or in the simple substance is nothing other than what one calls *perception,* which should be distinguished from apperception, or consciousness, as will be evident in what follows. This is where the Cartesians have failed badly, since they took no account of the perceptions that we do not apperceive. This is also what made them believe that minds alone are monads and that there are no animal souls or other entelechies. With the common people, they have confused a long stupor with death, properly speaking, which made them fall again into the Scholastic prejudice of completely separated souls, and

74. Deleted from earlier drafts: "and if simple substances were nothings, the composites would reduce to nothing."
75. Cf. "On Nature Itself," sec. 13, AG 163–65.

they have even confirmed unsound minds in the belief in the mortality of souls.[76]

15. The action of the internal principle which brings about the change or passage from one perception to another can be called *appetition;* it is true that the appetite cannot always completely reach the whole perception toward which it tends, but it always obtains something of it, and reaches new perceptions.

16. We ourselves experience a multitude in a simple substance when we find that the least thought we ourselves apperceive involves variety in its object. Thus, all those who recognize that the soul is a simple substance should recognize this multitude in the monad; and Mr. Bayle should not find any difficulty in this as he has done in his *Dictionary* article, "Rorarius."[77]

17. Moreover, we must confess that the *perception,* and what depends on it, is *inexplicable in terms of mechanical reasons,* that is, through shapes and motions. If we imagine that there is a machine whose structure makes it think, sense, and have perceptions, we could conceive it enlarged, keeping the same proportions, so that we could enter into it, as one enters into a mill. Assuming that, when inspecting its interior, we will only find parts that push one another, and we will never find anything to explain a perception. And so, we should seek perception in the simple substance and not in the composite or in the machine. Furthermore, this is all one can find in the simple substance—that is, perceptions and their changes. It is also in this alone that all the *internal actions* of simple substances can consist.

18. One can call all simple substances or created monads entelechies, for they have in themselves a certain perfection (*echousi to enteles*); they have a sufficiency (*autarkeia*) that makes them the sources of their internal actions, and, so to speak, incorporeal automata (sec. 87).

19. If we wish to call *soul* everything that has *perceptions* and *appetites* in the general sense I have just explained, then all simple substances or created monads can be called souls. But, since sensation is something more than a simple perception, I think that the general name

---

76. For Leibniz's critique of Descartes on the immortality of the soul, see the "Letter to Molanus," AG 240–45.

77. Leibniz's *Theodicy* was, to a large extent, an attempt to answer the skeptical arguments, from Bayle's *Historical and Critical Dictionary*, regarding the impossibility of reconciling faith with reason. "Rorarius," an article of the *Dictionary*, was Bayle's occasion for a discussion of the problem of the souls of animals: Jerome Rorarius (1485–1566) wrote a treatise maintaining that men are less rational than the lower animals. In "Rorarius" Bayle criticizes Leibniz's views; see Bayle, "Rorarius," notes H and L.

of monad and entelechy is sufficient for simple substances which only
have perceptions, and that we should only call those substances *souls*
where perception is more distinct and accompanied by memory.

20. For we experience within ourselves a state in which we remember
nothing and have no distinct perception; this is similar to when we
faint or when we are overwhelmed by a deep, dreamless sleep. In
this state the soul does not differ sensibly from a simple monad; but
since this state does not last, and since the soul emerges from it, our
soul is something more (sec. 64).

21. And it does not at all follow that in such a state the simple
substance is without any perception. This is not possible for the
previous reasons; for it cannot perish, and it also cannot subsist
without some property [*affection*], which is nothing other than its
perception. But when there is a great multitude of small perceptions
in which nothing is distinct, we are stupefied. This is similar to when
we continually spin in the same direction several times in succession,
from which arises a dizziness that can make us faint and does not
allow us to distinguish anything. Death can impart this state to
animals for a time.

22. And since every present state of a simple substance is a natural
consequence of its preceding state, the present is pregnant with the
future (sec. 360).

23. Therefore, since on being awakened from a stupor, we apperceive
our perceptions, it must be the case that we had some perceptions
immediately before, even though we did not apperceive them; for a
perception can only come naturally from another perception, as a
motion can only come naturally from a motion (secs. 401–403).

24. From this we see that if, in our perceptions, we had nothing
distinct or, so to speak, in relief and stronger in flavor, we would
always be in a stupor. And this is the state of bare monads.

25. We also see that nature has given heightened perceptions to
animals, from the care she has taken to furnish them organs that
collect several rays of light or several waves of air, in order to make
them more effectual by bringing them together. There is something
similar to this in odor, taste, and touch, and perhaps in many other
senses which are unknown to us. I will soon explain how what occurs
in the soul represents what occurs in the organs.

26. Memory provides a kind of sequence in souls, which imitates
reason, but which must be distinguished from it. We observe that
when animals have the perception of something which strikes them,
and when they previously had a similar perception of that thing,
then, through a representation in their memory, they expect that

which was attached to the thing in the preceding perception, and are led to have sensations similar to those they had before. For example, if we show dogs a stick, they remember the pain that it caused them and they flee (Prelim., sec. 65).

27. And the strong imagination that strikes and moves them comes from the magnitude or the multitude of the preceding perceptions. For often a strong impression produces, all at once, the effect produced by a long *habit* or by many lesser, reiterated perceptions.

28. Men act like beasts insofar as the sequence of their perceptions results from the principle of memory alone; they resemble the empirical physicians who practice without theory. We are all mere Empirics in three fourths of our actions. For example, when we expect that the day will dawn tomorrow, we act like an Empiric,[78] because until now it has always been thus. Only the astronomer judges this by reason (Prelim., sec. 65).

29. But the knowledge of eternal and necessary truths is what distinguishes us from simple animals and furnishes us with *reason* and the sciences, by raising us to a knowledge of ourselves and of God. And that is what we call the rational soul, or *mind*, in ourselves.

30. It is also through the knowledge of necessary truths and through their abstractions that we rise to *reflective acts*, which enable us to think of that which is called "I" and enable us to consider that this or that is in us. And thus, in thinking of ourselves, we think of being, of substance, of the simple and of the composite, of the immaterial and of God himself, by conceiving that that which is limited in us is limitless in him. And these reflective acts furnish the principal objects of our reasonings (*Theod.* Preface *.4.a).

31. Our reasonings are based on *two great principles, that of contradiction,* in virtue of which we judge that which involves a contradiction to be false, and that which is opposed or contradictory to the false to be true (sec. 44, 169).

32. And *that of sufficient reason,* by virtue of which we consider that we can find no true or existent fact, no true assertion, without there being a sufficient reason why it is thus and not otherwise, although most of the time these reasons cannot be known to us (sec. 44, 196).

33. There are also two kinds of *truths,* those of *reasoning* and those of *fact.* The truths of reasoning are necessary and their opposite is impossible; the truths of fact are contingent, and their opposite is possible. When a truth is necessary, its reason can be found by

---

78. The Empirics were a sect of physicians before Galen (ca. A.D. 150). In later times, the epithet "Empiric" was given to physicians who despised theoretical study and trusted tradition and their own experience.

analysis, resolving it into simpler ideas and simpler truths until we reach the primitives (sec. 170, 174, 189, 280–282, 367, Abridgment, objection 3).

34. This is how the speculative *theorems* and practical *canons* of mathematicians are reduced by analysis to *definitions*, *axioms* and *postulates*.

35. And there are, finally, *simple ideas*, whose definition cannot be given. There are also axioms and postulates, in brief, *primitive principles*, which cannot be proved and which need no proof. And these are *identical propositions*, whose opposite contains an explicit contradiction.

36. But there must also be a *sufficient reason* in *contingent truths*, or *truths of fact*, that is, in the series of things distributed throughout the universe of creatures, where the resolution into particular reasons could proceed into unlimited detail because of the immense variety of things in nature and because of the division of bodies to infinity. There is an infinity of past and present shapes and motions that enter into the efficient cause of my present writing, and there is an infinity of small inclinations and dispositions of my soul, present and past, that enter into its final cause (sec. 36, 37, 44, 45, 49, 52, 121, 122, 337, 340, 344).

37. And since all this *detail* involves nothing but other prior or more detailed contingents, each of which needs a similar analysis in order to give its reason, we do not make progress in this way. It must be the case that the sufficient or ultimate reason is outside the sequence or *series* of this multiplicity of contingencies, however infinite it may be.

38. And that is why the ultimate reason of things must be in a necessary substance in which the diversity of changes is only eminent, as in its source. This is what we call *God* (*Theod*. sec. 7).

39. Since this substance is a sufficient reason for all this diversity, which is utterly interconnected, *there is only one God, and this God is sufficient*.

40. We can also judge that this supreme substance which is unique, universal, and necessary must be incapable of limits and must contain as much reality as is possible, insofar as there is nothing outside it which is independent of it, and insofar as it is a simple consequence of its possible existence.

41. From this it follows that God is absolutely perfect—*perfection* being nothing but the magnitude of positive reality considered as such, setting aside the limits or bounds in the things which have it. And here, where there are no limits, that is, in God, perfection is absolutely infinite (*Theod*. sec. 22; *Theod*. Preface, sec. 4.a).

42. It also follows that creatures derive their perfections from God's influence, but that they derive their imperfections from their own nature, which is incapable of being without limits. For it is in this that they are distinguished from God (*Theod.* sec. 20, 27–31, 153, 167, 377 et seq.; sec. 30, 380, Abridgment, objection 5).[79]

43. It is also true that God is not only the source of existences, but also that of essences insofar as they are real, that is, or the source of that which is real in possibility. This is because God's understanding is the realm of eternal truths or that of the ideas on which they depend; without him there would be nothing real in possibles, and not only would nothing exist, but also nothing would be possible (*Theod.* sec. 20).

44. For if there is reality in essences or possibles, or indeed, in eternal truths, this reality must be grounded in something existent and actual, and consequently, it must be grounded in the existence of the necessary being, in whom essence involves existence, that is, in whom possible being is sufficient for actual being (sec. 184, 189, 335).

45. Thus God alone (or the necessary being) has this privilege, that he must exist if he is possible. And since nothing can prevent the possibility of what is without limits, without negation, and consequently without contradiction, this by itself is sufficient for us to know the existence of God *a priori*. We have also proved this by the reality of the eternal truths. But we have also just proved it *a posteriori* since there are contingent beings, which can only have their final or sufficient reason in the necessary being, a being that has the reason of its existence in itself.

46. However, we should not imagine, as some do, that since the eternal truths depend on God, they are arbitrary and depend on his will, as Descartes appears to have held, and after him Mr. Poiret.[80] This is true only of contingent truths, whose principle is *fitness* [*convenance*] or the choice of the *best*. But necessary truths depend solely on his understanding, and are its internal object (sec. 180, 184, 185, 335, 351, 380).

47. Thus God alone is the primitive unity or the first [*originaire*] simple substance; all created or derivative monads are products, and

---

79. The following appears in the second draft, but is missing in the final copy: "This *original imperfection* of creatures is noticeable in the *natural inertia* of bodies."
80. For Leibniz's critique of Descartes's concept of God, see the "Letter to Molanus," AG 240–45. Pierre Poiret (1646–1719) was initially one of Descartes's followers; he published a book of reflections on God, soul and evil, *Cogitationum rationalium de Deo, anima, et malo libri quattuor* (1677), which was attacked by Bayle.

are generated, so to speak, by continual fulgurations of the divinity from moment to moment, limited by the receptivity of the creature, to which it is essential to be limited (sec. 382–391, 398, 395).

48. God has *power*, which is the source of everything, *knowledge*, which contains the diversity of ideas, and finally *will*, which brings about changes or products in accordance with the principle of the best (sec. 7, 149, 150). And these correspond to what, in created monads, is the subject or the basis, the perceptive faculty and the appetitive faculty. But in God these attributes are absolutely infinite or perfect, while in the created monads or in entelechies (or *perfectihabies*, as Hermolaus Barbarus translated that word)[81] they are only imitations of it, in proportion to the perfection that they have (sec. 87).

49. The creature is said to *act* externally insofar as it is perfect, and *to be acted upon* [*patir*] by another, insofar as it is imperfect. Thus we attribute *action* to a monad insofar as it has distinct perceptions, and *passion*, insofar as it has confused perceptions (*Theod*. sec. 32, 66, 386).

50. And one creature is more perfect than another insofar as one finds in it that which provides an *a priori* reason for what happens in the other; and this is why we say that it acts on the other.

51. But in simple substances the influence of one monad over another can only be ideal, and can only produce its effect through God's intervention, when in the ideas of God a monad rightly demands that God take it into account in regulating the others from the beginning of things. For, since a created monad cannot have an internal physical influence upon another, this is the only way in which one can depend on another (*Theod*. sec. 9, 54, 65, 66, 201, Abridgment, objection 3).

52. It is in this way that actions and passions among creatures are mutual. For God, comparing two simple substances, finds in each reasons that require him to adjust the other to it; and consequently, what is active in some respects is passive from another point of view: *active* insofar as what is known distinctly in one serves to explain what happens in another; and *passive* insofar as the reason for what happens in one is found in what is known distinctly in another (sec. 66).

53. Now, since there is an infinity of possible universes in God's ideas, and since only one of them can exist, there must be a sufficient reason for God's choice, a reason which determines him towards one thing rather than another (*Theod*. sec. 8, 10, 44, 173, 196 & seq., 225, 414–16).

---

81. Hermolaus Barbarus (1454–93) was an Italian scholar who attempted, through retranslations of Aristotle, to recover Aristotle's original doctrine from under the layers of Scholastic interpretations. His works include popular compendia of ethics and natural philosophy, drawn from the writings of Aristotle.

54. And this reason can only be found in *fitness,* or in the degree of perfection that these worlds contain, each possible world having the right to claim existence in proportion to the perfection it contains (sec. 74, 167, 350, 201, 130, 352, 345 & seq., 354).[82]

55. And this is the cause of the existence of the best, which wisdom makes known to God, which his goodness makes him choose, and which his power makes him produce (*Theod.* sec. 8, 78, 80, 84, 119, 204, 206, 208; Abridgment, objection 1, objection 8).

56. This interconnection or accommodation of all created things to each other, and each to all the others, brings it about that each simple substance has relations that express all the others, and consequently, that each simple substance is a perpetual, living mirror of the universe (sec. 130, 360).

57. Just as the same city viewed from different directions appears entirely different and, as it were, multiplied perspectively, in just the same way it happens that, because of the infinite multitude of simple substances, there are, as it were, just as many different universes, which are, nevertheless, only perspectives on a single one, corresponding to the different points of view of each monad (sec. 147).

58. And this is the way of obtaining as much variety as possible, but with the greatest order possible, that is, it is the way of obtaining as much perfection as possible (sec. 120, 124, 241 & seq., 214, 243, 275).

59. Moreover, this is the only hypothesis (which I dare say is demonstrated) that properly enhances God's greatness. Mr. Bayle recognized this when, in his *Dictionary* (article "Rorarius"), he set out objections to it; indeed, he was tempted to believe that I ascribed too much to God, more than is possible. But he was unable to present any reason why this universal harmony, which results in every substance expressing exactly all the others through the relations it has to them, is impossible.[83]

60. Furthermore, in what I have just discussed, we can see the *a priori* reasons why things could not be otherwise. Because God, in regulating the whole, had regard for each part, and particularly for each monad, and since the nature of the monad is representative, nothing can limit it to represent only a part of things. However, it is true that this representation is only confused as to the detail of the whole universe, and can only be distinct for a small portion of things, that is, either for those that are closest, or for those that are greatest

---

82. The following appears in the second draft: "Thus there is nothing that is completely arbitrary."
83. See note to sec. 16, above.

with respect to each monad, otherwise each monad would be a divinity. Monads are limited, not as to their objects, but with respect to the modifications of their knowledge of them. Monads all go confusedly to infinity, to the whole; but they are limited and differentiated by the degrees of their distinct perceptions.

61. In this respect, composite substances are analogous to simple substances. For everything is a plenum, which makes all matter interconnected. In a plenum, every motion has some effect on distant bodies, in proportion to their distance. For each body is affected, not only by those in contact with it, and in some way feels the effects of everything that happens to them, but also, through them, it feels the effects of those in contact with the bodies with which it is itself immediately in contact. From this it follows that this communication extends to any distance whatsoever. As a result, every body is affected by everything that happens in the universe, to such an extent that he who sees all can read in each thing what happens everywhere, and even what has happened or what will happen, by observing in the present what is remote in time as well as in space. "All things conspire [*sympnoia panta*]," said Hippocrates. But a soul can read in itself only what is distinctly represented there; it cannot unfold all its folds at once, because they go to infinity.

62. Thus, although each created monad represents the whole universe, it more distinctly represents the body which is particularly affected by it, and whose entelechy it constitutes. And just as this body expresses the whole universe through the interconnection of all matter in the plenum, the soul also represents the whole universe by representing this body, which belongs to it in a particular way (sec. 400).

63. The body belonging to a monad (which is the entelechy or soul of that body) together with an entelechy constitutes what may be called a *living being*, and together with a soul constitutes what is called an *animal*. Now, the body of a living being or an animal is always organized; for, since every monad is a mirror of the universe in its way, and since the universe is regulated in a perfect order, there must also be an order in the representing being, that is, in the perceptions of the soul, and consequently, in the body in accordance with which the universe is represented therein (sec. 403).

64. Thus each organized body of a living being is a kind of divine machine or natural automaton, which infinitely surpasses all artificial automata. For a machine constructed by man's art is not a machine in each of its parts. For example, the tooth of a brass wheel has parts or fragments which, for us, are no longer artificial things, and no

longer have any marks to indicate the machine for whose use the wheel was intended. But natural machines, that is, living bodies, are still machines in their least parts, to infinity. That is the difference between nature and art, that is, between divine art and our art (sec. 134, 146, 194, 483).

65. And the author of nature has been able to practice this divine and infinitely marvelous art, because each portion of matter is not only divisible to infinity, as the ancients have recognized, but is also actually subdivided without end, each part divided into parts having some motion of their own; otherwise, it would be impossible for each portion of matter to express the whole universe (Prelim., sec. 70, *Theodicy*, sec. 195).

66. From this we see that there is a world of creatures, of living beings, of animals, of entelechies, of souls in the least part of matter.

67. Each portion of matter can be conceived as a garden full of plants, and as a pond full of fish. But each branch of a plant, each limb of an animal, each drop of its humors, is still another such garden or pond.

68. And although the earth and air lying between the garden plants, or the water lying between the fish of the pond, are neither plant nor fish, they contain yet more of them, though of a subtleness imperceptible to us, most often.

69. Thus there is nothing fallow, sterile, or dead in the universe, no chaos and no confusion except in appearance, almost like it looks in a pond at a distance, where we might see the confused and, so to speak, teeming motion of the fish in the pond, without discerning the fish themselves (Preface ***.5.b.* ***.b).

70. Thus we see that each living body has a dominant entelechy, which in the animal is the soul; but the limbs of this living body are full of other living beings, plants, animals, each of which also has its entelechy, or its dominant soul.

71. But we must not imagine, as some who have misunderstood my thought do, that each soul has a mass or portion of matter of its own, always proper to or allotted by it, and that it consequently possesses other lower living beings, forever destined to serve it. For all bodies are in a perpetual flux, like rivers, and parts enter into them and depart from them continually.

72. Thus the soul changes body only little by little and by degrees, so that it is never stripped at once of all its organs. There is often metamorphosis in animals, but there is never metempsychosis nor transmigration of souls; there are also no completely *separated souls*, nor spirits [*Génies*] without bodies. God alone is completely detached from bodies (sec. 90, 124).

73. That is why there is never total generation nor, strictly speaking, perfect death, death consisting in the separation of the soul. And what we call *generations* are developments and growths, as what we call deaths are enfoldings and diminutions.

74. Philosophers have been greatly perplexed about the origin of forms, entelechies, or souls. But today, when exact inquiries on plants, insects, and animals have shown us that organic bodies in nature are never produced from chaos or putrefaction, but always through seeds in which there is, no doubt, some *preformation*, it has been judged that, not only the organic body was already there before conception, but there was also a soul in this body; in brief, the animal itself was there, and through conception this animal was merely prepared for a great transformation, in order to become an animal of another kind. Something similar is seen outside generation, as when worms become flies, and caterpillars become butterflies (sec. 86, 89; Preface ***5.b. ff; sec. 90, 187, 188, 403, 86, 397).

75. Those *animals*, some of which are raised by conception to the level of the larger animals, can be called *spermatic*. But those of them that remain among those of their kind, that is, the majority, are born, multiply, and are destroyed, just like the larger animals. There are but a small number of Elect that pass onto a larger stage [*théatre*].

76. But this was only half the truth. I have, therefore, held that if the animal never begins naturally, it does not end naturally, either; and not only will there be no generation, but also no complete destruction, nor any death, strictly speaking. These *a posteriori* reasonings, derived from experience, agree perfectly with my principles deduced *a priori*, as above (sec. 90).

77. Thus one can state that not only is the soul (mirror of an indestructible universe) indestructible, but so is the animal itself, even though its mechanism often perishes in part, and casts off or puts on its organic coverings.

78. These principles have given me a way of naturally explaining the union, or rather the conformity of the soul and the organic body. The soul follows its own laws and the body also follows its own; and they agree in virtue of the harmony pre-established between all substances, since they are all representations of a single universe (Preface ***6; sec. 340, 352, 353, 358).

79. Souls act according to the laws of final causes, through appetitions, ends, and means. Bodies act according to the laws of efficient causes or of motions. And these two kingdoms, that of efficient causes and that of final causes, are in harmony with each other.

80. Descartes recognized that souls cannot impart a force to bodies because there is always the same quantity of force in matter. However,

he thought that the soul could change the direction of bodies. But that is because the law of nature, which also affirms the conservation of the same total direction in matter, was not known at that time. If he had known it, he would have hit upon my system of pre-established harmony (Preface ****; *Theod.* sec. 22, 59, 60, 61, 63, 66, 345, 346 & seq., 354, 355).

81. According to this system, bodies act as if there were no souls (though this is impossible); and souls act as if there were no bodies; and both act as if each influenced the other.

82. As for *minds* or rational souls, I find that, at bottom, what we just said holds for all living beings and animals, namely that animals and souls begin only with the world and do not end any more than the world does. However, rational animals have this peculiarity, that their little spermatic animals, as long as they only remain in this state, have only ordinary or sensitive souls. But that as soon as the Elect among them, so to speak, attain human nature by actual conception, their sensitive souls are elevated to the rank of reason and to the prerogative of minds (sec. 91, 397).

83. Among other differences which exist between ordinary souls and minds, some of which I have already noted, there are also the following: that souls, in general, are living mirrors or images of the universe of creatures, but that minds are also images of the divinity itself, or of the author of nature, capable of knowing the system of the universe, and imitating something of it through their schematic representations [*échantillons architectoniques*] of it, each mind being like a little divinity in its own realm (sec. 147).

84. That is what makes minds capable of entering into a kind of society with God, and allows him to be, in relation to them, not only what an inventor is to his machine (as God is in relation to the other creatures) but also what a prince is to his subjects, and even what a father is to his children.

85. From this it is easy to conclude that the collection of all minds must make up the city of God, that is, the most perfect possible state under the most perfect of monarchs (see 146, Abridgment, Objection 2).

86. This city of God, this truly universal monarchy, is a moral world within the natural world, and the highest and most divine of God's works. The glory of God truly consists in this city, for he would have none if his greatness and goodness were not known and admired by minds. It is also in relation to this divine city that God has goodness, properly speaking, whereas his wisdom and power are evident everywhere.

87. Since earlier we established a perfect harmony between two

natural kingdoms, the one of efficient causes, the other of final causes, we ought to note here yet another harmony between the physical kingdom of nature and the moral kingdom of grace, that is, between God considered as the architect of the mechanism of the universe, and God considered as the monarch of the divine city of minds (sec. 62, 74, 118, 248, 112, 130, 247).

88. This harmony leads things to grace through the very paths of nature. For example, this globe must be destroyed and restored by natural means at such times as the governing of minds requires it, for the punishment of some and the reward of others (sec. 18 & seq., 110, 244, 245, 340).

89. It can also be said that God the architect pleases in every respect God the legislator, and, as a result, sins must carry their penalty with them by the order of nature, and even in virtue of the mechanical structure of things. Similarly, noble actions will receive their rewards through mechanical means with regard to bodies, even though this cannot, and must not, always happen immediately.

90. Finally, under this perfect government, there will be no good action that is unrewarded, no bad action that goes unpunished, and everything must result in the well-being of the good, that is, of those who are not dissatisfied in this great state, those who trust in providence, after having done their duty, and who love and imitate the author of all good, as they should, finding pleasure in the consideration of his perfections according to the nature of genuinely *pure love*, which takes pleasure in the happiness of the beloved. This is what causes wise and virtuous persons to work for all that appears to be in conformity with the presumptive or antecedent divine will, and nevertheless, to content themselves with what God brings about by his secret, consequent, or decisive will, since they recognize that if we could understand the order of the universe well enough, we would find that it surpasses all the wishes of the wisest, and that it is impossible to make it better than it is.[84] This is true not only for the whole in general, but also for ourselves in particular, if we are attached, as we should be, to the author of the whole, not only as the architect and efficient cause of our being, but also as to our master and final cause; he ought to be the whole aim of our will, and he alone can make us happy (sec. 134 end, Preface *4.a.b.; *Theodicy*, sec. 278, Preface *.4.b).

---

84. The distinction between God's antecedent and consequent will can be found in Thomas Aquinas, *Summa Theologiae* I, q. 19, art. 6, ad 1.

Brief Biographies of Some Contemporaries of Leibniz

ARNAULD, Antoine (1612–94), was a philosopher and mathematician, though primarily a theologian (associated with the Jansenist movement). He was first a critic of Cartesian philosophy, writing the "Fourth Set of Objections" to Descartes's *Meditations* (1641), but later he became one of its proponents. He carried on a significant philosophical correspondence with most of the principal thinkers of the seventeenth century. His main works include the Port-Royal *Logique* (with Pierre Nicole—1662) and *Des vraies et des fausses idées* (1683), a work dealing with Malebranche's thought, which set off a lengthy and important controversy.

AVERROISTS were followers of Averroes (Ibn Ruschd, 1126–98), who held that the active intellect in each individual human soul is part of a single active intellect to which one is reunited in death.

BARBARUS, Hermolaeus (1454–93), was an Italian scholar who attempted, through retranslations of Aristotle, to recover Aristotle's original doctrine from under the layers of Scholastic interpretations. His works include popular compendia of ethics and natural philosophy, drawn from the writings of Aristotle.

BAYLE, Pierre (1647–1706), was the editor and founder of the *Nouvelles de la République des Lettres*, a review of new books, in which frequent reference to Leibniz's works could be found. In 1695–96, he published the *Dictionaire Historique et Critique*, a precursor to the encyclopaedist movement of the eighteenth century. The *Dictionary* was extremely influential.

BOYLE, Robert (1627–91), was a physicist and chemist, a prolific author whose main contributions were researches on the elasticity of the air and the air pump. Moreover, he was instrumental in the popularization of experimental science and the corpuscular theory, against the natural philosophy of Aristotle and Scholasticism. Among his works were *New experiments physico-mechanical, touching the spring of air* . . . (1660), *The Sceptical Chymist* (1661), and *The origine of forms and qualities* . . . (1666).

COSTE, Pierre (1668–1747), was the French translator of English philosophical works, including John Locke's *Essay* in 1700. He corresponded with Leibniz and acted as a channel between Leibniz and Locke.

DESCARTES, René (1596–1650). It would be difficult to overstate the importance of Descartes's work for any aspect of seventeenth-century intellectual life: for mathematics and optics—the *Geometry*, *Optics*, and *Meteorology*, the essays appended to his *Discourse on Method* (1937); for natural philosophy, biology, and geology—the *Principles of Philosophy*, Parts II, III, and IV (1644); for metaphysics, epistemology, and philosophical psychology—the aforementioned *Discourse*, the *Meditations on First Philosophy* (1641), and the *Passions of the Soul* (1648).

FLUDD, Robert (1574–1637), was a follower of Paracelsus who maintained, in his *Philosophica Mosaica* (1638), that the true philosophy has been revealed by Moses and could be extracted from the Old Testament, especially the Pentateuch.

HOBBES, Thomas (1588–1679), was an English philosopher and mathematician. By Leibniz's own account, Hobbes was a great influence on him in his early years. Hobbes's most important works are the *Leviathan* (1651) and the *De corpore* (1655).

LOCKE, John (1632–1704), was an English philosopher whose fame rests mainly on his *Essay Concerning Human Understanding* (1690) and *Two Treatises on Government* (1690). The *Essay* underwent numerous stages: early manuscripts are dated 1671; the manuscript seems to have reached final form by 1686; Locke published a summary of it in France in 1688; there were editions with substantial revisions in 1690, 1694, 1695, 1700, and posthumously in 1706. Coste's French translation was published in 1700, and a Latin translation, in 1701.

MALEBRANCHE, Nicholas (1638–1715), the great Cartesian and exponent of occasionalism, is best known for his *Search after Truth*, published in 1674; also significant are the *Traité de la nature et de la grâce* (1680), *Méditations chrétiennes* (1683), *Dialogues on Metaphysics* (1688), and *Traité des lois de la communication des mouvements* (1692).

MASHAM, Lady Damaris (1658–1708), was a correspondent of Leibniz's. She maintained an important circle of philosophers, scientists, and theologians. Locke lived at her house during the final years of his life. Coste was her son's tutor.

QUIETISTS were followers of Miguel de Molinos (ca. 1640–97) and others who stressed passive contemplation and complete resignation to the will of God.

SCALIGER, Julius Caesar (1484–1558), was a Renaissance scholar, a translator of Greek and Latin works, and the author of a Latin grammar.

SNELL, Willebrord (1581–1626), was a naturalist, physicist, and optical theorist who published . . . *De re nummaria liber singularis* (1613), a work on money, and . . . *Tiphus batavus, sive histiodromice, de navium cursibus, et re navali* (1624), some lessons on navigation. His best-known discovery, of the laws of the refraction of light, was probably formulated in 1621 and described in a now lost manuscript.

SPINOZA, Baruch (1632–77), was a philosopher. He published little during his lifetime, but his posthumously published *Ethics* was extremely important and provocative.

STILLINGFLEET, Edward (1635–99), Bishop of Worcester, attacked Locke's *Essay*, in his *Discourse on the Vindication of the Trinity* (1696); Locke defended himself in a *Letter* (1697), eliciting a reply from Stillingfleet (1697), thereby eliciting a further defense from Locke— *Reply to Worcester's Answer . . . to His Letter* (1697)—these were followed by another reply from Stillingfleet (1698) and Locke's *Reply to . . . Worcester's Answer to His Second Letter* (1699).